SPI
EGE
L&G
RAU

COAL TO DIAMONDS

COAL TO DIAMONDS

A MEMOIR

BETH DITTO

WITH MICHELLE TEA

SPIEGEL & GRAU   NEW YORK

Published in the United States by Spiegel & Grau, an imprint
of The Random House Publishing Group, a division of
Random House, Inc., New York.

Spiegel & Grau and Design is a registered trademark of
Random House, Inc.

Library of Congress Cataloging-in-Publication Data
Ditto, Beth.
Coal to diamonds: a memoir/Beth Ditto; with Michelle Tea.
p. cm.
ISBN 978-0-385-52591-6
eBook ISBN 978-0-385-52974-7
1. Ditto, Beth.   2. Punk rock musicians—United States—
Biography.   3. Lesbian musicians—United States—Biography.
I. Tea, Michelle.   II. Title.
ML420.D5665A3   2012
782.42166092—dc22   2009051672
[B]

Printed in the United States of America on acid-free paper

www.spiegelandgrau.com

2 4 6 8 9 7 5 3 1
First Edition

Book design by Liz Cosgrove

Dedicated to my two families: the family I was born into and the family I chose. You all give me a purpose, a history, and a future. You all keep me driven, inspired, and laughing. I never meant any of these stories to put anyone in a bad light; they are all true, some painful. Without *all* the stories, the best ones and the worst ones, I wouldn't be who I am now. I'm proud of myself—something I can say because of all the people in this book.

In memory of my dad,
Homer Edward Ditto
1954–2011

COAL TO DIAMONDS

1

There was a time when Judsonia, Arkansas, was a booming metropolis keeping pace with the rest of the country. The people were hopeful—working, shopping, and living life. A women's college was teaching ladies, and the town cemetery kept a plot for fallen Union soldiers right smack in the middle of all the dead Confederates.

That was back in the 1940s. Then in '52 a tornado swirled in and tore the whole place down, leaving a dusty depression in its wake. After that, time got sticky while the people got slower and stayed that way. Since then, Judsonia just hasn't moved on the way the rest of the country has.

At thirteen years old, I was hanging out one afternoon in a pair of sweats and a hand-painted T-shirt, bumming around a mostly empty house. It was the early '90s, but there, in Judsonia, it might as well have been the '80s, or the '70s. I, Mary Beth Ditto, did not go to school that day. I stayed at home to laze around the house—a house that was normally crawling with way too many kids and a sick aunt, but which was miraculously empty that day, totally peaceful. Just because I played hooky, don't go getting the idea that I was a bad kid. I wasn't, but I wasn't a good kid either. I wasn't a nerdy square turning in homework on time and kissing my teacher's butt, and I certainly wasn't some juvenile delinquent ducking class to hunt down trouble. I just wanted to see what that big, hectic house would feel like full of unusual quiet.

My three little cousins were off at school. Because they had the misfortune of being born to the world's shittiest mom, those three cousins—who all had names that began with A—had come to live with Aunt Jannie. When social services had finally been called for the fourth time, the social workers poked around to see if those three little A's had any family who could take them in, and when they found Aunt Jannie she, of course, said yes.

The A's made their beds on couches and chairs at Aunt Jannie's, crawling next to one another in the night, hunkering down wherever there was space and warmth to snuggle into. Their arrival in Aunt Jannie's home was part of a grand tradition in my family. In a family so large that it tumbled and stretched to the edges of comprehension, every one of us came knocking on Aunt Jannie and Uncle Artus's front door eventually, looking for refuge. Something always pushed us there. For the A's it was their drunken, neglectful mother. For me it was my violent stepfather. For my mother it was her sexually abusive father. And there were countless other short-term squatters, like my cousins whose mother shot her husband in the head. Children came and children went as circumstance and tragedy dictated. Aunt Jannie just couldn't turn away a kid with nowhere to go, not even when her diabetes made her so slowed-down and sickly.

Aunt Jannie took people in for so many years that her house probably would've felt empty without stray bodies on every spare bit of furniture. Jannie's heart—her original heart—was a good and giving thing, even though her life had fossilized pain around the outside. Deep inside, Jannie was secretly warm and caring, and that was the place that made her take in any person who was

going through a tough time in life. She never sat down and calcu-
lated the costs of being the whole town's savior. Her impulse to
help, plus the whole town's expectation that she would open her
doors, and everyone loving her for doing it, meant that, eventually,
Aunt Jannie just couldn't say no to anyone. Even when maybe she
should have. When she was at the end of her mental rope, Aunt
Jannie probably needed someone to reach out and give her a hand,
but I don't know how she could've asked for that when she was the
one always giving it.

Aunt Jannie's daughter—my Aunt Jane Ann—lived in that big
house too. Jane Ann was young enough to feel like a sister but old
enough to take me to a Rolling Stones concert. Her teenage son,
Dean, was the unofficial king of the house. While the rest of us
lived like forest creatures, constantly looking for a nice space to
burrow in, Dean got his very own bedroom. His own bedroom!
I couldn't comprehend the luxury. Like some put-upon fairy-tale
princess I earned my place keeping the A's in line and tending
to Aunt Jannie's slow-motion suicide—fixing her the pitchers of
Crystal Light that had her as addicted as the five packs of full-flavor
Winstons she smoked her way through each day. That was taking
care of Aunt Jannie: tearing open packets of the fake-flavor tea and
inhaling the lemony aspartame powder till my nose was crusted
with it, then bringing it to the kitchen table, where she lit her Winstons one from another. There was always something smoldering
in the ashtray. I would sit in the cigarette haze and listen to her talk
about the old times in Judsonia. Truth be told, being an audience
for Aunt Jannie's crazy tales was my real task; they could snag
my imagination better than television. I would listen, wide-eyed,
to her outlandish stories, like the ones about her running from
her wheelchair-bound mother as a little girl and climbing up on
the furniture so that poor woman, who was crippled from polio,
couldn't grab her. Aunt Jannie was a spitfire Scorpio. She used to
sneak down to the river, to a chained-up shed that hid a forbidden
jukebox. Judsonia didn't allow dancing, so Aunt Jannie, thirteen

years old and full of pent-up fire and life, would sneak into the woods with other barely teenage rebels, and together they'd dance, getting drunk on home-brewed liquor and twirling away the night.

That teenage Aunt Jannie felt her culture pushing down on her, and so she pushed back with the shove of her whole body twisting to the beat. In between segments of *Wheel of Fortune* and *Jeopardy!* she told me all about it. Aunt Jannie always got the answers to all the game shows right, smacking the table with satisfaction when they confirmed her answer. She would've won big bucks as a contestant, but she wasn't, so she was just smart, the smartest, a genius, always guessing that phrase before Vanna White flipped the vowels over, or getting the answer before that schoolteacher from Omaha hit the buzzer. Aunt Jannie had the smarts—she was even good at math—but she'd dropped out of school when she was just fourteen. As much as I didn't care about school, I couldn't comprehend being forced to drop out because I'd gotten pregnant and lost the father—my love—in a crashed-up car on a country road. That was Aunt Jannie's story, and it was mine to imagine back then, to bear witness to.

As the reigning teenage king of the house, Dean didn't have to hang with Aunt Jannie or corral the three little ones. He didn't have to try to keep the wild mess of the house under some sort of control or clean up after the two mangiest dogs ever, Alex and Cleo—little froofy mutts. Dean didn't have to deal with any of it, he just hung out in his room like royalty. He was a year older than me, and even shorter than me, five foot three at best.

Dean was a pool shark. Still a kid, trolling the pool halls, he'd wager with grown men and come home with a wad of cash balled up in the front of his Levi's: twenty, twenty-five dollars. That's a lot when you're a teenager in Judsonia. He blew his winnings on weed, tall glass bongs tucked in his closet, and cases of something strong to get drunk on with his friends in the woods. As for the Izods and Eastlands, loafers and Levi's—the preppy-popular look Dean rocked so well—his mom, Jane Ann, put all that on credit cards. A credit card wardrobe and a room all his own. Dean had it made.

The afternoon that I'd skipped school, I was watching television in the kitchen, half missing the constant chatter of Aunt Jannie and her suffocatingly familiar cloud of smoke while I flipped through the stations. My aunt's shabby immune system had allowed a staph infection to bloom in her body, so Jane Ann had gone with her to the hospital for antibiotics. Some dork in a suit was cleaning up on *Jeopardy!* If Aunt Jannie were there she'd have kicked his butt. *What is the quadratic equation? What is plutonium? Who is Eleanor Roosevelt?* Then Dean walked in, doing something violent to a Coke can.

What are you doing, Dean? I asked, watching him stab tiny holes into the aluminum with a knife.

Makin' a pipe.

A pipe? On the screen, Alex Trebek confounded the contestants with a new question; in the kitchen I watched my cousin's odd crafting, stumped.

For pot, he explained. The can was crushed, almost folded. On the far end, away from the opening, Dean poked and punctured until he'd created a tiny perforated area for a clump of weed to be ignited, then inhaled through the mouth of the can.

I'd never thought of a Coke can in quite that way before, and I guess it was sort of nice to observe Dean engaged in something remotely useful.

You want to smoke some? he invited. It wasn't like Dean to share the wealth, so I figured I should take advantage of his generosity. Besides, smoking pot with Dean seemed much more exciting than spacing out to another round of *Jeopardy!* I tagged behind my cousin.

Something you should know about that hectic house filled with aging, chain-smoking party girls, young moms and younger kids, with crazy puppies and me—the misfit cousin/built-in babysitter/housekeeper/nurse—is that the house was built from the ground up by Uncle Artus himself. Uncle Artus was an excellent carpenter and had made a bunch of money supervising jobs around the state of Arkansas. He just must have been so crazy busy with paid work that he never quite got around to finishing up his own place. Though he'd built it thirty years before, most of the fixtures in the house still hung from wires. The windows were just frameless panes of glass stuck into the walls, unfinished. A person could see straight into the outdoors through cracks in the joints, especially when it started getting colder and the wood contracted. That day it was chilly, autumn, so the cracks grew wide and the whole house got colder. I shivered in my sweats and my favorite T-shirt—Aunt Jannie had painted a chanteuse on the front of it with fabric paint, a glamorous lady coming out of a giant seashell. Back then there weren't many things I could call my own. I didn't have a bed, and many mornings I rifled through Jane Ann's dresser in search of clean bras and underwear. But that T-shirt was mine, and so was the character on it: a singer, a girl.

Like the rest of the house, Dean's room was a mess. His bed was a knot of blankets, and dirty clothes littered his floor. I leaned against the open window and tried to seem cool. I'd never smoked pot before. It didn't seem like a terribly bad thing to do—certainly more innocent than hard drugs that made people into zombies, or even getting drunk off a bottle of whiskey. But it was a bigger, badder deal than smoking a cigarette, and smoking a cigarette is all I'd ever done. An old babysitter had taught me to inhale at the tender age of six. That unethical babysitter—she was on the clock taking care of me the day she got herself knocked up—taught me how to pull the smoke into my lungs, and I'd been smoking ever since. I fed my habit by slipping Winstons from Aunt Jannie's pack during our talk-and-television marathons. But marijuana belonged to a whole new tier of inebriants. I watched as he suctioned his face to the can, releasing smoke out the window with ease, and I followed his lead. I angled my mouth against the hole in the can while Dean dipped a lighter onto the scrabble of charred weed.

The smoke poured into my lungs in a hot gust. If cigarette smoke was a windy day, this was the tornado that sacked Judsonia. I swallowed it, choked, and felt my eyes burn and turn runny. I was concerned about looking like a baby in front of Dean, but he wasn't paying me any mind. He was already singeing the rest of the weed and taking a final, powerful hit. He pursed his lips like Mick Jagger around the exiting smoke while I waited to feel the effects of the pot, and waited. I felt a little dizzy, but maybe that was from the coughing fit? I took an inventory of my body and mind. Then my cousin dropped the ashy can on his bedroom floor and reached for his gun.

In Arkansas, it's no big whoop to have guns lying around. If you don't have guns in your house, folks are apt to think there's something not quite right about you. My friends' families had cabinets where guns gleamed, displayed like porcelain figurines on a mantel. In Dean's pigsty, his .22 rifle was just leaning casually against the wall by his bed. While I was in my stoned reverie, Dean leaned out the window and *pop pop pop* took down a trio of squirrels in the time it took me to think, Whoa, dude. The tiny mammals fell from their perch, landed on the ground, and sent up a kick of dust around their fur. The same skills that made Dean a kick-ass pool player also made him an excellent shot. Precision and a steady hand, depth perception, angles and physics, and a spot-on instinct for when to shoot, to send the eight ball rolling toward the corner pocket or knock that squirrel out from its tree. It didn't hurt that the backyard was teeming with squirrels. Shit too. Out back was a little trail that led to an open sewer at the edge of the woods. If someone in the house flushed the commode you could watch the shit rush out of the pipe and into this ditch and it would float away, to where I don't know. My cousins and I would be playing out back, where wild mulberry bushes and pecan trees grew. Bunches of the nuts fell from the trees, and what we couldn't gnaw open we'd toss into the open sewer, trying to sink the shit that bobbed there.

Newly stoned, my body felt grimy and cold. I needed a hot shower. Dean ran out to the yard to collect his kills and I took further advantage of the empty house, luxuriating in the hot water without anyone yelling at me to hurry up, hollering that they had to pee or take a shower themselves, and nobody bitching about the cost of hot water. Compared to the poverty of the home I'd run away from—well, "run away" is too dramatic, I'd just found a reason to leave, and no one stopped me—Aunt Jannie's house was positively lower-middle-class. They had multiple boxes of Kraft Macaroni & Cheese standing inside their cabinets. They had Little Debbie snack cakes, all kinds of chocolate delights harboring secret creamy middles, chocolate dunked in chocolate, tunnels of sweet peanut butter, and Aunt Jannie's favorites—chocolate-covered cherries. Aunt Jannie's house had credit cards backing it, so anything was possible—new appliances, guns, televisions, a bounty of groceries. But still, no one was rich, and the cost of hot showers for a household of eight added up. I toweled off, got back into my sweats and special chanteuse T-shirt, and walked out of the bathroom into the greasy, meaty stink of fried squirrel.

I had the munchies! Dean hooted from the kitchen table. The plate on the table in front of him was scarfed clean, a pile of leg bones and the dirty frying pan the only evidence of Dean's impressive stoner feat: nailing three squirrels with a shotgun, then skinning them out in the yard, cleaning the meat, and frying it up, all while high on some kind of bud smoked out of a Coke can.

Smaller than a chicken, bigger than a rat. I hadn't eaten squirrel since I was a kid, and it would take more than stoner munchies to get me to snack on it again, especially in a house stocked with Little Debbies and Doritos. I wasn't a vegetarian, but something about eating the animals that had been traipsing through the backyard moments before—squirrels, deer—started to gross me out as I got older. Hunting everyday mammals was as normal in Arkansas as the guns ornamenting everyone's houses. My dad liked to boil a squirrel head and suck the brains out the nose. Not my idea of gourmet, but nothing outrageous in Judsonia. Simply the sort of vaguely nasty food enjoyed by adult men where I'm from.

The tails, however, fit into my idea of a good time. While the squirrel skins and grisly innards were dumped in the yard to be picked away by scavengers (or Alex and Cleo), the tails were treasured like rabbit's feet—a bit of the wild in the palm of your hand, exotic and icky, lucky even, though not for the squirrel. Growing up, all the kids had squirrel tails; in the fall, when squirrel hunting peaked, they were everywhere. You'd carry them around and play with them until your mom decided they'd become too disgusting and threw them away. But before they got too ratty they were sleek and soft, like a secret curled in your jacket pocket for you to snuggle your fingers into.

The pot wore off before I could really figure out whether or not it had done its job on me. Dean left his squirrelly dishes behind for me to clean up, and he took the stairs two at a time to seal himself inside his bedroom. Soon the three A's came home, and later Jane Ann, but Aunt Jannie, hadn't. Forty-seven years old, gone into the hospital for a staph infection and held there for lung cancer. I waited for her in the stale cigarette air of the kitchen, but things would never be the same again.

2

Because Aunt Jannie was tough and mean, it was always a comfort to be beside her. Imagine if a fearsome lion allowed you into her den and protected you there. You'd feel like the coolest person ever—chosen by a lion, a beast that munches other people to bloody ribbons, but not you. There must be something so special and excellent about you that secures you the lion's protection. That's how it was with Aunt Jannie and me. Aunt Jannie was cruel enough to scare the dark away, but she was never cruel to me. It was a shaky sort of safety, but our standards of safety were so low that we felt protected in situations like that, and I thought I was.

Aunt Jannie was always too hot; she'd sweat like she had a coal furnace in her guts stoking her. She'd crank up the air-conditioning in April to try to keep cool, but it wasn't enough. She found clothes unbearable. She'd take everything off and sit around in her bra and this underwear called Lovepats that were real stretchy and came up high around her middle. Lovepats were so cool, high-waisted granny chic.

Aunt Jannie in her underwear wasn't like some lady hanging

out in her bra and panties who was too lazy to get dressed or trying to be sexy. She wasn't trying to be shocking either, but if you were shocked, that was your problem, not hers. That mixture of comfort and defiance was her claiming the right to be comfortable inside her body and her home, with just the right amount of fuck-you, and it fascinated me just as much as her undergarments did.

Entitled: that's what Aunt Jannie was. Entitled to her own body, entitled to its comfort, entitled to live in her home as if it was hers. I think about her home, with all those people in it, and maybe lounging around in Lovepats was a way Aunt Jannie reminded herself she was the queen. She sat around in her underwear and nobody could say a goddamn thing about it.

Aunt Jannie didn't sit quietly in her Lovepats, either. She'd let out with a curse word as the inspiration struck her, and inspiration struck quite frequently. *Cocksucker, motherfucker.* I learned classic, shocking swearwords from Aunt Jannie, and I took them with me to the schoolyard, outrageous words that became just another tool in my arsenal. My town was tough, and Aunt Jannie was teaching me how to take up space and keep people away. Saying the shocking thing first made people a little scared. Who knew what I'd do? Are you going to mess with the fat woman sitting in her underwear and cursing in her kitchen? I do not think you would.

I was always discovering something more about Aunt Jannie. Just when I thought I had the whole of her figured out I'd learn a swearword or hear a new story. The day I learned about the tittie rock, I'd been balancing on a kitchen chair, hunting for a box of Teddy Grahams on top of the refrigerator.

What's this? I asked, holding out a long, strange rock the size and weight of a roll of quarters, with grooves worn into it for fingers to clutch.

Oh, you don't know what that is? Aunt Jannie grinned, teasing and proud. She waited for my answer.

A rock? I guessed stupidly.

You're half right. She smiled. I clambered down from the chair with the rock in one hand and a box of cookies in the other. Aunt Jannie took the rock and wrapped her hand around it. The rock disappeared in her hand, but Aunt Jannie's fist looked heavy and strong.

It's a tittie rock! she crowed. *It's for punching girls in the titties.*

Like Lara Croft with her giant gun or the goddess Athena with her sword, Aunt Jannie had a signature weapon. A tittie rock. Aunt Jannie fought a lot when she was younger. I couldn't imagine she was still punching girls in the titties when I discovered her rock, and she was older and sick, but she kept the thing around just in case.

As she got older things shifted a bit. Even though Aunt Jannie had a special weapon for women, she hated men the most. Aunt Jannie was the first man-hater I'd ever met, outwardly harshing on the whole bunch of them, not shy about it either. Cocksucker and motherfucker. She wasn't spitting those insults about women. Aunt Jannie could size up a man in seconds, be it an arrogant brainiac on a game show or the family's no-good man of the moment. I knew that Aunt Jannie's radar for "cocksuckers" and "motherfuckers" had been honed through her lifetime. No one knew, exactly, what man or men had done what to Aunt Jannie. Women in Judsonia didn't talk about such things. All that was certain was that something dropped a layer of cement over that heart of hers. Something made her hard and scary. My guess is if you did a lineup to see who was responsible, a whole mess of ghosts would emerge from the past. Even though I was young I already knew how to stay quiet about the things men and boys did to me, I knew how to get up and keep going in spite of it, but what I didn't know was how to be sharp and mean, protective and fierce, full of fuck-yous and defiance. That was what Aunt Jannie taught me.

3

With a Southern accent it's hard to say anything in a single syllable. Speech is sort of lazy and luxurious, like the speaker needs to wring every possible bit of sound from a word and let it linger in the humid air. With a Southern accent a one-syllable word becomes two-syllabled. You can stick an "ay" in there somewhere, stretch that short, stumpy word into something melodic. *Jane* becomes *Jayayne*. Like the mouth can't let go of the language, and the tongue just wants to hold on to the sound of it for a second longer.

It's hard to say one-syllable words with my accent; I have to avoid them entirely if I can. No abbreviations for me. A mic is always a microphone. A bike has to be a bicycle. Sorry if your name is Mike, 'cause I'm gonna have to call you Mikey. Maybe Michael if you make a fuss. Another way to deal with the problem of the single-syllable name is to just throw another name at the end of it. Lee becomes Lee Lee. Jane becomes Jane Ann. June becomes June Bug. And then there is the way the accent renders a name unrecognizable, or turns it into another name entirely. Take my mom's name, Velmyra. Folks call her Myra, but for years my paternal granny thought her name was Maura. The woman was shocked when she saw my mother's birth certificate. She'd been calling her daughter-in-law by the wrong name all those years, and no one else had picked up on it.

Let me tell you about my mother, Velmyra Estel—Velmyra after her granny Velvie May (whose twin brother was named Elvie Ray, of course) and Estel after her granny Estel Robinson. At some point in my mother's childhood, my grandma looked at my mother and said, *Well, you're the other woman.* My grandma learned about her husband's abuse of her daughter and didn't even get upset about it, let alone press charges. She would have almost certainly left it alone if her friend and confidante hadn't said to her, *You need to take your girl to the doctor; you never know what she might have, now.* And so she did. Once in the doctor's office, the situation flew out of my grandmother's hands and into the hands of the state. That's how my mother found herself, not yet a teenager, sitting in a courtroom as a judge decided whether or not her father had raped her.

The intense sexism, the male privilege that no one even recognized as such, were simply the way things were, the way things had always been and would always be in Arkansas. White man's rule was not questioned or challenged, especially by some twelve-year-old girl telling stories about her very own father. In a place where so many men were abusive, the whole system operated to deny the existence of abuse, to make it normal, unpunishable.

The trial lasted from the time my mother was twelve and a half to the time she was fifteen and a half. The whole town knew about it, and hardly anyone was on my mother's side. School was unbearable. The local newspaper ran a story mistakenly naming my mother's brother as the accused. Rumors were everywhere and she felt like there was nowhere to turn.

People came to the courthouse to testify against my mother. My grandma took my mother and her little brother—my uncle—and the three of them fled to Aunt Jannie's. But the night before the hearing, Grandma slipped away and met with her accused husband at a hotel room. His lawyers were hiding out on the street, snapping pictures of her as she came and went, and they brought those pictures before the judge. *Your Honor, here is a photo of this man's wife, the girl's own mother, leaving a hotel with him this very morning! Why would she stand beside him—sleep beside him!—if he was guilty of the horrible things he is being accused of?* Maybe because she was schizophrenic, for starters. Maybe because the violence in her household had been so severe for so long that the most awful things became normal. My grandparents' relationship was really tumultuous long before the courts were involved. My grandmother once grabbed a gun and went after her husband, intending to kill him. Her son, still just a kid, got in her way. *If you're going to protect that bastard I'll shoot you too,* she'd told him.

My grandmother wasn't the only one who went after that man with the intent to kill. Some years earlier, my mother had done the same thing. Never imagining anyone would care about the abuse she was experiencing, or that an adult who was interested in protecting her would appear and intervene, Velmyra decided to murder her father. She had a knife—not a gun—a weapon suited to her size, in her ten-year-old hand. She couldn't have handled the weight of a rifle, or the kick of it; she didn't like weapons and was a terrible shot. But knives are sneaky, and they can be hidden and whipped out at the perfect moment. Walking down the hallway toward the room where her father sat, my mother suddenly heard a voice, the raspiest voice she ever heard. *Go ahead,* it said to her, and she knew the voice belonged to the devil himself. *You'll feel better,* it urged; *he'll be gone.* Velmyra *would* feel better. Her body would be hers again, maybe; her nights would be hers, her house would be hers, maybe even her life would be hers. But another voice swooped in, not an ugly voice at all, something smooth, golden. *Don't do it,* it counseled. *It won't make anything better.* In the dark hallway, my mother was having a vision. That sweet voice was God, and he was battling the devil over the state of her soul. The devil's voice rang through Velmyra's mind; he goaded her forward. But something was fending him off; it was God himself, she knew it to be. It was pure love, sweet and tough, and protectiveness too. The good voice filled her, drowning out the evil rasp. My mother lingered in the hallway, her hand slick with nerves, wrapped around the knife. She was exhausted and teeming with fear. She listened to the good voice; she fought the devil. In the end, the devil vanished. He was simply gone, absorbed into nothingness. And then God was gone too, but she could feel his warmth upon her. She retreated down the hallway, flinging the knife beneath her bed.

Maybe that environment was why my grandma couldn't separate the sort-of bad from the really bad from the unthinkable, and maybe it was why she was capable of pulling a gun on her husband over a random argument but then spent the night with him the night before his trial for raping their daughter.

The whole world was against Velmyra Estel during her trial. She had to sit in the courtroom with no one but her lawyer on her side. She must have felt so small. People came and testified against my mom and called her a liar in the courtroom. The judge did not rule in her favor, so her lawyer gave her the best advice he could, in that time and place: *Get yourself married and get out of that house, don't look back.* My mother left the courtroom and moved herself into Aunt Jannie's house. Then she waited for some man to come for her so she could have a home of her own again.

Two years after my mom tried to kill her father, when she was just twelve years old, she was condemned as a liar by a judge. That morning, just a girl, she listened to her lawyer's advice to find a man and fix her situation. One would come, she was certain. Meanwhile she'd bide her time at Aunt Jannie's, where mess and chaos ruled, but where she slept unmolested.

She wouldn't have to wait so long. When she was fifteen, Velmyra Estel married a man named Homer Ditto. By the time she was twenty-four, she'd had three of Homer's babies—my big brothers, Benny and Robbie, and my sister, Akasha—but there was no more Homer. Their split wasn't too messy—Homer stayed in the picture, wanting to be a father to his children. Mom found another man, not for long but long enough to have his baby, number four, Mary Beth Ditto. My mother gave me Homer's name and let me think he was my biological father. He was back in the picture soon enough and didn't mind taking me on, and it was probably too sad and exhausting to tell me the truth anyway. I was just a kid, and Homer was as much of a dad as I ever had. So he gave me his name and I became Beth Ditto. Most people think it's a punk name I made up when I joined a band, but it's the truth. Mary Beth Ditto, born February 19, daughter of Velmyra and Homer.

Mom went on to have more husbands and more kids after Homer—my little brother Jacob, and my baby sister Kendra— which isn't strange in Arkansas. Women there have plenty of children before their heads stop spinning from their own bewildering childhoods. I wouldn't change my big, crazy, loving family for anything in the world, but women in Judsonia never had a break to catch their breath or to think about what the hell had happened to them and just let some sort of adult perspective emerge. Growing up there is fast and harsh. Young women pull a bunch of children into the world behind them, without a rest for their brains or their bodies, or their hearts. No space to understand the abuse that had happened, never mind time to figure out how to unlearn what they didn't even know they'd been taught, or to have a fighting chance to break the cycle. There are just babies upon babies, each one a link in a chain that connects back to the past; the legacy of abuse is made so normal you feel you have to move halfway across the country to come out from under the spell of where you're from. I got out eventually. But first, I had to get through Arkansas.

4

My mother's reputation in Judsonia is complicated. She is an extremely likable woman, affectionate, capable of keeping everyone, including herself, in a fit of wild giggles. She is a warmhearted Sagittarius, and a really funny person, goofy as hell.

To this day, in my family, Halloween is like Christmas. Like seventy-five people show up to celebrate, just from our family. We have hayrides and weenie roasts and bob for apples out in woodsy Georgetown. There aren't many cops in Georgetown, so we can pile twenty kids on a tractor and drive them illegally up and down the river and not get caught. My mother was always so funny on Halloween. Everybody loved her. Kids loved her. She was *that* mom, the one everyone wanted as their own. She lived for those adoring kids and loved them right back.

My mother loved dressing up so much that one Easter—she couldn't even wait for Halloween—she dressed up as a bunny and went to work. She was wearing a full-on bunny costume, thinking it was so funny, but she's a nurse who works with old, delirious people. The patients started reporting to the doctors that there was a huge white rabbit walking around, the size of a person. The doctors took notes about those old people having a psychotic break until one of them finally spotted my mother, jovial as hell, bopping around in her bunny costume.

Mom didn't drink or smoke pot or touch cigarettes. Her mother smoked cigarettes during her pregnancy—at her doctor's recommendation!—and as a result, Velmyra Estel was born with severe developmental lung problems. She's never even tried a cigarette, and I still won't smoke in front of her.

Affectionate and kind, pure in her habits, my mom was regarded by the town as a modern-day witch because she was different, significantly so in a place where guns are kept as casually as pets and where white people use the N-word so frequently their kids think it's just another harmless word. But Velmyra was different. As she still likes to say, *Homey don't play that.* My friends freaked out when they learned they weren't allowed to spit the N-word in my home; it was probably their first experience of resistance to racism—of even recognizing racism. My friends also thought it was bizarre that we didn't have a single gun stashed in my house, not even a regular old hunting rifle. Mom wouldn't allow it. She'd lived through way too much violence to ever feel comfortable around weapons. How could she look at one and not remember her mother threatening to shoot her brother?

But that wasn't the only thing that set us apart from the rest of Judsonia. Mom filled a vital role in the town. Judsonians would ignore her in the street, but when their daughters became pregnant (or decided to make an effort to not get knocked up) it was my house those girls were brought to and my mother who took them in for abortions and birth control. Mom fought violence, racism, and sexism in her own ways, in the small spaces where she was allowed control as a single mom in 1980s Arkansas, and this inconsistent yet very determined strength was enough to get her branded as a witch. If that was witchy, so be it.

When I was a little kid, if you asked me what I wanted to be, I would say a nurse, same as my mom. It made sense that my mom didn't indulge in unhealthy vices; she worked hard keeping other people healthy, and she tried to keep herself healthy too. Except she dieted. Mom was always on a diet, and her diets got more extreme when she was between men. After my father left, her body got smaller and smaller. She chopped all her hair off into a cute, wild style, started wearing Converse, and disappeared for days at a time. By the time I started high school, Mom, who had once been the size I am now, had starved herself down to a size zero. She was vanishing before our eyes.

It didn't help that there was never anything to eat in the house. As far back as I remember, we never had food in the cupboards and never a telephone to call for help when our hunger became scary. One summer Mom left my big sister Akasha in charge of baby number five, a newborn. No money in her pockets, nothing but her genuine charm and desperation to barter with, Akasha set out on the long walk to the country store, the sun smacking down on her little head. She was just a girl, trying to figure out how to ask the man at the store to give her some milk so she could make her baby brother shut up.

Of course the man wanted to know, where was our mother? Our mother was working. She was doing her best to keep a roof over our heads and was desperately working as much as she could to put something in those bare cupboards.

I remember Akasha stoic, her teeth gritted against tears. Too proud to weep in front of the country-store clerk, even if her tears might have been the thing to break him down and get him to hand over a gallon of milk. I remember Akasha coming up the road with nothing in her hands, the baby wailing on my lap in the shade of the porch. I jiggled my knees, trying to soothe his cries with the motion, but nothing would work except food. Akasha was mute with rage, her jaw clamped shut around feelings too big for her body. What sort of monster lived inside my big sister? Some beast of hurt and anger, fear and injustice, some animal made of pure weariness she kept inside. She climbed the porch steps, and her empty hands said everything. Akasha guzzled some water from the tap and then hiked over to see Aunt Jannie, who always had a cup of milk for us and would probably throw some Little Debbie snack cakes into a bag as well—a marshmallow pie or cupcake encased in waxy chocolate. That's just the backward way girls grew up in my family: daughters shouldering burdens, becoming baby adults. Aunt Jannie didn't ask questions, Aunt Jannie didn't even blink, she just poured the milk into a piece of Tupperware and sent Akasha on her way, hustling back home before the Arkansas sun turned the milk sour.

5

When I was around twelve, my mother had a boyfriend, Gary the sound man, who lived in mythical Little Rock, a place where people had universal indoor plumbing and private telephone lines. They were allowed to dance in Little Rock, unlike in Judsonia, where dancing had been outlawed a million years before and no one's spirit was intact enough to challenge it. Judsonians danced in their rooms, or in the shower beneath the spray, or some of us snuck into the forest in search of an outlaw jukebox. Little Rock might as well have been New York City for all its comparative sophistication.

When Gary came to Judsonia for a visit it was like a living, breathing piece of cool came into our home. Everything looked small and shabby next to Gary, who twitched with unease in our seriously uncool house. The carpet felt more worn and everything seemed even less cool than it had been before Gary showed up. Maybe Gary was so powerfully cool he sucked the pathetic smidgeons of cool out of every lousy place he visited. Gary had long hair like a Ramone and round glasses perched on his face. I wanted him to like me so badly, but he didn't.

Gary was really into blues music, which was the first music I found myself crazy obsessed with. I was super into Lead Belly, who'd become king of twelve-string guitar playing in the brothels of Shreveport, Louisiana. Lead Belly had done time in the slammer, worked a chain gang for carrying a gun and stabbing a white guy in a brawl. *I was over in Arkansas,* he sang. *People ask me what you come here for.* Good question, Lead Belly!

I loved Ma Rainey, the Mother of the Blues. Ma Rainey might have even been the one who named the whole soul-creaking, heart-seizing style of sad, mad music "the blues." She traveled the vaudeville circuit and was scandalously bisexual. In the '20s she got arrested for throwing a wild party where all the ladies were naked with one another. I tried to impress Cool Gary from Little Rock with my vast knowledge of these important musicians, chattering on and on like a baby Ken Burns. Gary looked briefly at my mother and then fixed his gaze on me, asking, *Don't you ever shut up?* I gave it a bit of serious thought. Did I ever shut up?

I don't, actually, I said truthfully. *I guess I don't shut up.*

He scoffed at me and shook his head, his hair swinging up into his face. He cleaned his eyeglasses on his T-shirt and turned to my mother. *What's there to do around here, huh?* Like a kid trapped visiting his parents in some dead-end suburb, Gary was over Judsonia and he was over me and my blues babbling.

And I was over Gary, no matter how cool he was, no matter how infused with big-city glamour, dancing and smoking and loud, loud music. His affair with my mother ended after his visit to Judsonia, and I wonder if the reality of my mother's life—a future of inevitable visits back to soul-crushing Judsonia, where he'd be set upon by a gang of unruly brats—was just too much for him.

At first I was glad when Mom stopped seeing Gary and was spending more time at the house. When she left us alone my fear of the dark, always strong and constant, flared wider, seemed to eat me whole. My fear of the dark is an honest-to-God phobia. My body forgets it knows how to breathe and the guillotine of panic comes down on all air passages. If I'm in a dark room and have to walk across the length of it to reach the light switch, I count the seconds in my head to try to calm myself. I can never believe how long it takes as the darkness pushes against the numbers: 1, 2, 3, 4. The phobia ruins my sleep, gets in the way of most anything that occurs at night. Having my mother back in the house was a comfort, but just because she wasn't rushing off to Little Rock every night didn't mean she'd initiated a new era of order and calm.

Mom's dieting, a constant, got worse. My mother always suffered from a distorted body image. With Gary out of the picture and no new guy on the horizon, she fed herself less and less. She got bursts of high, manic energy as her body went into actual starvation—an evolutionary survival tweak designed to give you the gusto to go club a deer. My mother used it at work, making her rounds with a creepy speed and purpose, her body jutting and angular and increasingly unfamiliar. She grew more talkative but made less sense. Her body turned on itself, harvesting its own muscles for protein. People stopped telling her she looked great and started asking her if she was okay; their voices were concerned. It was a only matter of time before her body gave out beneath her, with no more evolutionary tricks up its sleeve. She collapsed one day and was taken to the hospital. My mother had always had a normal, healthy female body. But by the time she went to the hospital, her body had shrunk to something pitiful.

No one, including her doctors, ever acknowledged that my mother was starving herself. My mother never realized what she was doing. Was it for the men? Because every single thing in this world sunk the message, deeply, that skinny was pretty, fat was ugly, and if you want a man—and Mom did—you'd better be skinny. Did it give her a sense of control to master deprivation? Did she get addicted to the secret rituals of starvation, feel proud that at least one unruly thing in her life was under her management?

Or maybe my mother was simply used to putting herself last. A person can get used to taking nothing. My little brother used to save her the crusts of bread because he thought they were her favorite, but my mother just insisted on giving us everything she had and living on whatever was left over. Even hunger, acute hunger, can start to feel so normal you don't notice it. I'll never know why Mom let her body get so emaciated that it stopped working, because she doesn't like to talk about that. All I know is that my mom continued to party once she got out of the hospital.

It was another couple of months before she settled down. There were a lot of whirlwind romances. Men came and went, which was fine for my mom, but it wasn't so good for her daughters, who were right in the middle of their formative years.

Mornings brought their own discomfort as Mom, whose understanding of what was appropriate got messed up so young, recounted the details of her one-night stands as if Akasha and I were her girlfriends. We sat at the table one morning while a one-night stand dropped her off. We weren't her daughters but her confidantes. I felt a nameless, itchy feeling—a bad one—that was all mixed up with another feeling: happy that my mother was happy, happy and home, not in the hospital, not away in the dark but there in the light with us. My mother's attention was spread so thin that I never got much of it, so there was something perversely sweet about those mornings, acting like high school girls gossiping after a night of sneaking out to meet boys in the woods.

With my mother trying to reclaim some lost youth, and my sister and me aged by our own shitty circumstances, we met in some inappropriately teenage middle. My mom often flung herself into a kitchen chair, taking off her jacket to reveal just a bra underneath, worn like a shirt. I was always bleary from a night of bad sleep, waking in the darkness only to have to fight off the terror of it. Now I felt myself resisting a different dark feeling—that it was wrong to know so much about what my mother was doing out there with the men she met.

This is where life got really confusing, where Mom's coming and going turns into a blur. Too scared to sleep in the dark house without any grown-ups around, I stayed at Aunt Jannie's more and more. Life got less and less stable, and I found myself living nowhere but staying everywhere: my mother's house sometimes, Aunt Jannie's sometimes, depending on how many others were staying; my dad Homer's sometimes, when I could handle sleeping all the way out in Georgetown—so rural it made Judsonia look sophisticated. If you're feeling confused about where I was when, believe me, so was I. I was a transient in my own family, often sleeping in a different house every night.

Moving back and forth among so many houses, I didn't feel like I belonged anywhere. If anyone asked me where I lived I didn't know what to say. *Here and there, I guess.* There was nothing to anchor me to any house. I didn't have a dresser anywhere, but it didn't matter, since I didn't own enough clothing to fill one. I remember one bountiful teenage Christmas getting a winter coat and a pair of jeans thanks to Aunt Jannie. They, along with my love-worn Pearl Jam T-shirt, were the only pieces of clothing I could truly call my own, since by that time my puffy-paint chanteuse shirt was too threadbare to wear and wound up shredded into cleaning rags, stored under Aunt Jannie's kitchen sink. At the start of high school I really had nothing—no home, no clothes, and no idea how messed up my situation really was.

6

Every so often Mom would totally surprise me by deciding to act like a real mom. An overprotective-type mother who wanted me around, wanted to know where I was, kept an eye on things. Although I partly longed for that type of mothering, once I got it I didn't know what to do with it. I didn't trust it. I knew my mother would only be able to keep her motivation up for a minute, and then men, or life's chaos, would take her attention back and I'd be left with less of her than before. And if my mother didn't quite know how to be a mother, at that point I didn't really know how to be a daughter.

My mother had a new friend from work, Jo Ann, who, seeing my mom struggle with her unruly kids, tried to help out the best way she knew how. Jo Ann set Mom up on a blind date with some guy named Mike. Two weeks after they met, I came home from school and watched him lugging his shit through my mother's front door. I stopped in my tracks as I clambered off the school bus, watching the man's movements, confused. *Is this the right house? Do I live here?* I was easily disoriented with all the moving around. Then I saw Akasha and my brothers peeking out at the guy as he pulled trash bags and boxes over the threshold.

You comin' or goin'? asked the annoyed bus driver, and I climbed out of the bus and into my new family.

This is Mike, Mom introduced him as I maneuvered my way around his stuff. Behind me Mike continued lugging his things into our home.

Later that night, Mike made us dinner. Spaghetti. It could have been homey, if it wasn't so creepy. When you think about what teachers have to go through to work with kids, getting finger-printed and whatnot, when you think about how a professional nanny arrives with references and background checks, it's baffling that any lady can just move any old blind date into her home, a scant two weeks' acquaintance suddenly stepdad to a posse of kids. Over my spaghetti I shot Mom a look that was stuffed with unspo-ken accusations and pissed-off bewilderment. She gave me a look in return and I dropped my gaze to my pasta. I knew what Mom's look was telling me: *Dry it up.* That was her number-one favorite phrase. The mom who was so cool and understanding when my friends came over, freaking out about their fucked-up families, vanished when it came to her own kids. She shut herself down and demanded we do the same. *Dry it up.* I heard her voice in my head as easily as if she'd spoken out loud, but Mom wasn't talking. She was controlling us kids with significant glances, picking at the edges of her spaghetti and smiling sweetly, thankfully, at Mike the Blind Date.

It was around this time that my mother told me Homer Ditto was not my father. Nope. Mom had had a fling with some other guy who was my dad. Some dude who didn't stick around too long, who Mom was happy to get rid of. She chose Homer, and Homer chose me, so he lent me his name even though I didn't have his blood. Now, you might think that finding out I was an illegiti-

mate child was a big deal, but there is so much mixing and matching where I come from, families spilling over into other people's
houses, what's yours gets determined by what feels right, not by
anything technical. Dad was the guy who'd been nicest: Homer
Ditto.

Probably Mom would have let me think forever that Homer
was my bio-dad if my actual birth father hadn't stepped in with
an out-of-the-blue desire to be paternal. The man lived in Rockford, Illinois, and when he'd asked my mother what sort of a gift
I'd like, the first thing that popped into her mind was something
from the Rockford Peaches, and a signed baseball showed up at
our home soon thereafter.

One of my most favorite movies is *A League of Their Own*, about
the Rockford Peaches, the first professional female baseball team.
They were women in the 1940s who stepped up to play baseball
while all the men were off fighting the war. Everyone thought they
were big jokes. But they were tough and talented and knew there
was no crying in baseball.

I was happy to have that signed baseball, but I—along with everyone else in my family—was not interested in letting my birth
father back into my life.

The span of time my mom spent with my birth dad was a great
and terrible era. Great because I was born. Terrible because the
man who'd knocked Mom up was violent and awful. No one understood why my mother had left good-natured Homer to be with
my bio-dad. He often took his fury out on my brothers, Homer's
kids. The constant meanness and physical brutality he'd inflicted
on them as kids stuck in their minds. In my home his name in-
voked hatred, and suddenly he was trying to come back around,
calling Mom on the phone and sending me the best gift I'd ever
gotten.

It never made any sense for me to feel responsible for the
abuse my brothers suffered. I was a newborn baby at the time,
and who knows what crappy conditions I was suffering through,

long and blissfully forgotten. Still, the man who'd so famously hurt my brothers belonged to me. He was my birth father, and someone who was connected to me had done that. I felt ashamed, and scared. I didn't want to be a traitor to my brothers. When my bio-dad called, I pretended I wasn't home. I never called him back, and it didn't take many dead ends for the guy to quit trying. Soon enough he was relegated to the land of bad memories, his name only uttered if needed, and always with venom. Homer was my dad anyway, in the real way that matters. I was happy to keep his name and he was happy to keep me as his daughter.

But the baseball. I couldn't get rid of that baseball. It wasn't the baseball's fault my bio-dad was a worm.

Not long after Mike moved in, my brothers moved out. Soon Mike left too, in a choppy fashion. Back and forth, coming and going, their on-again, off-again romance making me cry each time he slammed the front door out of our life. Mom thought I was crying because I'd become attached to him, but I was only scared about how my mother was going to pay the bills without him around. Mike and his extra money stabilized the household. Spaghetti dinners and snacks in the cupboard, milk in the fridge. I cried at the memory of Akasha looking for milk in the Arkansas summer. Then Mike came back long enough for baby number six to be on the way.

When Kendra—I got to name her—was born, Mom's household was at its weirdest and most tumultuous. Shortly after the baby's birth I found Akasha sitting on the porch, right where I had sat years before, rocking a different screaming baby, waiting for my big sister to return with his milk. Now she was rocking, a slight, pained rock, back and forth, her hands in her hair. I felt scared for her, tilting back and forth like that, anguished. I walked up to her, hesitant. Akasha and I were never warm or affectionate with each other, even though we were close. I was never her little sister or kid sister, just her sister.

"Akasha, what's wrong?" I almost didn't want to know.

"I can't believe Mom had another baby." Her long hair stuck to her wet face. She'd already lost most of her childhood to raising Mom's kids. Her summers weren't for friends or leisure, but for maintaining the crazy household of needy, hungry kids. Akasha had already given up sleepovers and her summer vacations to help raise Mom's kids. She was a little mom herself. That premature responsibility made Akasha into a really tough person, with a steel exterior she has to this day. She comes off as hard to get along with, but I understand her. Akasha is ready to go to the mat over any little thing anyone says to her. If you'd been through every-thing we had, you'd understand.

7

Under normal circumstances, a kid would be excited if her mother found happiness and stability, but Tom's entrance into our lives was not something that we kids were excited about. We didn't trust him.

Despite my mother's best efforts to be an accommodating wife and mother, my siblings and I weren't going to buy into her act. There were only four of us at home by then, and we'd been fending for ourselves for a while; we weren't looking for anyone to come in and start laying down laws.

After two weeks of my mother knowing Tom, he became her full-time *live-in-sin friend,* to put it in her words. It didn't take long to tell that Tom and I wouldn't see eye to eye.

Out of all the men in my life, there are some I love and some I loathe, and my worst fear was that I'd loathe Tom. Unfortunately that fear came true. I was afraid for my family, especially my younger brother and sister. I didn't want Kendra to turn eight and get a surprise visit from a stranger saying, *Hi, I'm your dad.* Not cool.

With Tom in the house, I felt like it was my time to leave. My mother wanted me to stay, even if I hated coming home. I found other places to stay as often as I could.

Sometime after Tom drove me out, my sister Akasha overheard him talking shit to my mother through their closed bedroom door: *She's your daughter but she has to go.*

Akasha fought with Tom and then left. She left proud because that's Akasha, but she was really thrown out by Tom, and Mom let it happen. Akasha went to live with her dad, Homer, out in Georgetown, and eventually got a place with our brothers.

Georgetown is located in a little nook in the bend of a river. There is one dusty road in and it's the same dusty road you take out. My grandmothers lived out there; one of them didn't get an inside toilet until the '80s, and the other continues to pump her own water. Up until the '90s, the town shared a single party phone line. You'd pick up the telephone and be smack in the middle of your neighbor's conversation. That town that hadn't budged since 1956 was where my sister was exiled to. Like my brothers, Akasha was a genius at math and science, always winning awards. She could do trigonometry stoned, with her eyes closed. Once she got sent away to Georgetown she started smoking a bunch of pot and skipping school. She still got straight A's, but something was different. There was no way Akasha was going to be satisfied stuck in the middle of nowhere with no way out.

Luckily, even though she was stuck in Georgetown, Akasha quickly learned to be resourceful. She hornswoggled my father into buying her a car so she could have her independence. I moved out to Georgetown with my dad and sister for a little while, but I was still fifteen with no license and no job—and too young to get either—so eventually I left and went to the only better situation I could find that was closer to home. However macabre it may sound, it was lucky for me that my Aunt Jannie had fallen ill, because it provided a serious enough reason for me to stay out of my mom's house without being exiled to Georgetown.

8

The time I spent living with my dad and sister was brief but hilarious. We watched the same VHS tape—no cable in Georgetown—of *The Simpsons* over and over until we could recite it by heart. Akasha and I smoked cigarettes and wrote excuses for each other to stay home from school. I was sad to say goodbye to my dad's place, but the bright lights of Judsonia beckoned.

So I moved in with my aunt, who, due to her neglected diabetes and the deplorable state of her home—the conditions there were perfect for a thriving disease—grew a huge staph infection on her ankle, leaving an opening for a free full-time nurse, a position I gratefully accepted. At the time, I was just looking for a way back to civilization, but I wasn't prepared to deal with everything I signed up for.

My little cousins—the three A's—were subjected to daily punishments that my aunt doled out. One of those young cousins, who had the misfortune of being the only boy, had to stand with his nose literally to the corner from the moment he got home from school until bedtime, with only a short break to eat. Since he was stuck in the corner most of his childhood you would never have known what a funny, likable kid he was. All the things he might enjoy were deemed bad for him and taken away one by one. He wasn't allowed sugar because he was "hyperactive." The cruelty he endured at home created an unmanageable monster in the eyes of his ill-informed caretakers, so his teachers took playtime at school away and class time became his only free time. Imagine if the only time you could relax was when you were able to sit at a desk and turn your head from side to side. I can't prove it, but there was suspicion that he wasn't getting his Ritalin. I lived in that house for two years and I only saw him get his medicine twice. With everything that was happening, he built up so much energy and anger. How could he have sat still in school? He needed an outlet.

That said, I think Aunt Jannie genuinely didn't understand what was going on. She was damaged, frustrated, and confused. None of that ever excused her behavior, but it does help to explain how she could be a hero and a villain at the same time.

At Aunt Jannie's I always had to clean up the dinner mess and try to keep the chaos under control. By that time, Aunt Jannie's sicknesses were getting the best of her body. Every evening, after we finished eating, she went to the couch to lie down while my cousin stood in the corner. He'd be there for so long that he couldn't help shifting from leg to leg. There was always fear in the air, and while I wanted my cousin out of the corner, I also wanted him to escape any worse punishment. I never knew how to help, or what to do. Aunt Jannie might have gotten up from the couch, and I didn't want her to see him disobeying, so I felt like I couldn't chance letting him roam free. The few times that I dared to speak up for him, we both wound up in serious trouble. That's just the way it was at Aunt Jannie's. I was so confused.

The fights with Tom at my mom's house were still fresh in my mind, and staying in Georgetown—as fun as it could be—didn't work for me. I found myself stuck in a bad situation that felt like a slightly better alternative to the other things I was running from.

Though Aunt Jannie had never laid a hand on me, she would holler and shut me out if I didn't do what she said. Her way of punishing me was to withhold her love and companionship, two things I was desperately seeking at the time.

My immediate family was extremely disconnected. My brother Benny was doing well. He was on tour, playing music all over the country. My other brother Robbie was living on his own and taking care of himself, and Akasha was trying to be the first high school graduate in our family. I was lost in the shuffle.

One night Aunt Jannie gave my cousin a whupping for putting too much water in the tub for his bath. He was only allowed one inch. I heard her yelling in the bathroom. I told myself it was just a spanking. Lots of kids got spanked, although how many kids do you know who were only allowed one inch of bathwater? It was becoming clearer and clearer that Aunt Jannie just had it out for him. I felt a creepy, no-good feeling coming on me, the awful feeling of something bad being true sinking in like a stone: Aunt Jannie was sabotaging my cousin.

Eventually, it became obvious that I couldn't stay much longer. All of us kids were scared of Aunt Jannie for different reasons— physically afraid or emotionally afraid—and I couldn't take it anymore. She was intimidating, incredibly smart, and, for Arkansas, she was a liberated, independent woman, which was both inspiring and frightening.

I really do believe my aunt started out a good person. If Aunt Jannie at twenty-one saw herself at forty-seven she wouldn't recognize that person. She had a lot to give, but maybe all the years of Aunt Jannie never getting to stop and think about herself made her twisted up inside. How long can a person tuck herself away like she's nothing, needing nothing, before she loses it? It seemed like everyone in my family was shelving bad secrets in the back of their minds. Aunt Jannie probably had hers; I'm sure she had hers. There must have been some memory that turned her into a monster, slowly polluting her heart.

Before I left Aunt Jannie's there was a string of curious inci-
dents. While my younger cousin was wild, he wasn't violent. Always affectionate, he was a sweet little boy by nature. So it came
as a surprise when Dean's bed had been slashed more than thirty
times with a steak knife and there was only one person who was
capable of doing it: that sweet little boy. But no one knew what
could have motivated him. There were enough sources of anger
and resentment, but until then nothing had pushed my little
cousin that far. We all just thought he'd had enough.

And then there was the ring—a shining example, literally, of
the hierarchy among my cousins. If it had been the dark ages my
little cousin wouldn't have been more than a serf and Dean was
definitely a king, so when Dean's ring disappeared we all heard
about it. Big gold rings were in, and someone's credit card had purchased a nice shiny one for Dean. Then the ring went missing—or
that was the story anyway. We never knew exactly how it happened, but it wound up with a little girl in my younger cousin's
class. You can imagine what her mother thought when she came
home with a 24-karat gold nugget ring. Her mother called Jane
Ann, and Dean went ballistic. Things were tense before, but they
seriously escalated after that call.

In hindsight, I can now say that what happened to my little
cousin in that house was abuse, absolute abuse. At the time, I
thought that "abuse" would be more violent, that there would be
more bruises, more welts, that it would be like an '80s after-school
special. The abuse in Aunt Jannie's house just felt like a constant
low-level hum, like the buzz of a refrigerator that you didn't even
notice because you'd adjusted to the sound so long ago. Growing
up with spankings, I just didn't see that behavior as abuse. Even
today, I still feel like spankings aren't so bad, that they aren't really
beatings. I'm numbed out to it. But that's the result of being ex-
posed to such constant, mundane abuse for so long.

The adults around me did nothing about the situation. Some
who tried to intervene watched it blow up in their faces, with Aunt

Jannie's rage and intensified punishments for my cousin. As for social services, I didn't even think about turning to the system for help. The system had demonized my mother when she was only twelve for looking to get rescued from her abusive father. After that, she didn't believe any child would be better off in the system, and I couldn't argue.

Needless to say, the situation at Aunt Jannie's was mentally and physically exhausting. Aunt Jannie went to the hospital frequently, and she also had routine trips to the doctor, so there was a little more peace in the house, but I missed her company and affection. On top of that, Jane Ann had taken to introducing me to people as her live-in babysitter maid instead of her relative. I had to ask her to stop. Feeling homeless and unwanted was rotten enough; to think that my family had stopped seeing me as family and had started thinking of me as some girl who cleaned up after them was terrible.

Even though staying at Mom's house sucked once she married Tom, sometimes I needed to go back and be with my mother. One of the things keeping me at Aunt Jannie's was literally dying, and the other three—the little A's—were too painful to watch anymore; my little cousin and his sisters only made me feel more helpless. So I stopped staying at Aunt Jannie's all the time and gave my mom's house another shot.

I was staying at Mom's when the phone rang one morning. It was one of my younger cousins, calling to tell us Aunt Jannie had died. I covered my mouth and looked at my mom, who instantly knew what I'd been told. We were shocked. Everything happened so quickly after Aunt Jannie got sick. The staph infection kept her in the hospital long enough for the doctors to figure out that she had cancer, and then Aunt Jannie was gone in what felt like a matter of weeks. It was my earliest lesson in real loss. There was nothing I could do. No amount of Crystal Light or chocolate-covered cherries could bring her back.

I went back to Aunt Jannie's. I wasn't sure if I could—or even wanted to—stay there without her. It felt like she was only in the other room, like you could find her resting in bed, wake her up to watch game shows, ask her to talk about the old days in Judsonia, dancing to outlaw jukeboxes in the woods. Aunt Jannie was mean, crazy mean, but I could only imagine the world had made her that way, that if I'd have had Aunt Jannie's life I could have easily become her: so much fury and no power to do anything with it.

After she died, I stood in her house, which still stunk like Aunt Jannie's cigarettes. Judsonia had made her. It had shaped the paths available to her; it had provided the punishments when she strayed; it had kept that wild Scorpio girl in some sort of shaky line. I hoped she was at peace, if peace was what she wanted. Maybe heaven for Aunt Jannie was a place where a woman could start a ruckus, speak her mind, and people would listen. When I thought about Aunt Jannie's heaven I just hoped that she was in a place where she could be free.

9

Aunt Jannie's place was a rough house for the three A's to grow up in. Though my little ADD cousin often got the worst of Aunt Jannie, his older sister didn't have it much better. For every bit of negative attention that her brother got, she got no attention at all. So it's no wonder no one noticed the awful thing she confided in me one day.

We were very close. I couldn't do anything about her brother's situation and their baby sister was only six months old when she showed up on Aunt Jannie's doorstep. I wouldn't say there are any upsides to being the firstborn, but there are definitely no upsides to being the first girl. We were close enough in age that we related to each other and got along, but we were far enough apart that I felt protective of her. It must have been similar to the way that Akasha felt about me.

One evening, she came to me while the house was almost empty. She wanted to talk to me about Dean. She said he was doing things to her. You could hear the shame in her voice. I don't think she was afraid to tell me, I just think she was embarrassed to say the words. I wasn't shocked, because Dean had asked me for a blowjob in the past, but I had just said no. What I understood was that what Dean was doing was sexual, not that it was sexual abuse. We were taught that predators were strangers luring pretty girls into vans with candy, or masked men in dark alleys covering your screams with gloved hands. Where were the examples of abuse within the family? We were all kids, me and Dean and my little cousins. What was going on between us couldn't be abuse, could it? It was a norm. At that point in my life I thought that we all—as kids—had to deal with some form of hurt.

When I was younger, I was bitter at my brother for the relationship he had with my Uncle Lee Roy. Lee Roy is a perfect example of the famously incestuous South: Aunt Nancy, who is married to Uncle Lee Roy, is my adopted dad Homer's sister. Uncle Lee Roy is also the brother of my birth father's grandmother. So regardless of which dad I wound up with, Uncle Lee Roy was destined to be part of my family. I hate that name, Lee Roy, and I hate that man. It's hard for me, because I look like him. I have his body—short and stocky—the same body as my grandmother. He was handsome-ish, with his hair slicked back into a pompadour. He wore thick, black glasses until the day he died. He worked at Wal-Mart, and I remember him most vividly in his Wal-Mart uniform. I can also remember some different outfits I had on when he cornered me; I can remember zoning out to the television while his hands gripped me, how I let my eyes lose their focus until the television was a kaleidoscope of shifting colors, the rise and fall of a laugh track. I remember a lot.

I would say Uncle Lee Roy was a creep. He oozed an inappropriate sexuality. Not all sexual abuse is about sex—it can be about power, humiliation, habit—but for Lee Roy in my heart I know it was about sex. Every time we were alone, his hands were everywhere. Down my pants, down my shirt. It was a normal experience—Uncle Lee Roy had been coming at me that way ever since I could remember, beginning when I was about four years old.

Then it got worse. I would sleep at his house. I don't know why everyone thought that was safe; Uncle Lee Roy had a reputation. My father lived with him for a while when I was five, and I would spend the night because one of my cousins lived there too. Their presence in the house didn't stop him. I remember once being in the living room while a whole pile of relatives were in the kitchen. Anyone could have just looked over and seen what he was doing to me, but I guess nobody did. When I stayed with my dad I would fall asleep in his bed but I'd wake up in the middle of the night to go to the bathroom or try to find a more comfortable spot to sleep. Lee Roy was a night owl.

I never wanted to kiss Lee Roy goodbye. In my family we kiss on the lips. I just couldn't do it. I would come home to Mom's house and I would be on fire. Below my belt would be on fire. I don't even know how it happened—how I got from one room to another, how I got home. I just remember fire.

My mother knew Uncle Lee Roy was a pervert; she talked about it all the time, how he had felt her up when she was young. Great-Uncle Lee Roy, he was like fourteen years older than Mom, a real old man. One afternoon Mom was talking about him, how he was a known sleaze. A familiar feeling came over me, and there, for the first time in our living room, I told her what had happened. Also for the first time, I saw it for what it really was. Mom froze when my words hit her. *Your dad better not have known about this.* Then she called him. But it didn't end then. When I was in third grade, one of my teachers tried to step in to stop the abuse too, but she did it so awkwardly it backfired, and I wound up feeling worse. Without meaning to, I told a friend from school that I was being abused. I was so young then, and though I knew what was happening was bad, I also thought it was normal, and so I felt confused a lot about what to talk about and what to keep hidden. The girl who I had unwittingly confessed to told her mother about it over dinner. The mother called our teacher and the teacher sat me down at recess. I thought I was in huge trouble. *I heard you did it with a guy,* she said—a pretty blunt, unknowingly insensitive way to put it. I was speechless. I denied it. I just froze. My teacher let me go out to recess, and I found a place in the schoolyard apart from the other kids and I sat there. I just sat there. It made me anxious for days to know that people knew. It didn't help, I only felt like I was in trouble.

Scared to death is how I felt after my teacher took me aside. I just felt like I'd been found out. How she said *I heard you did it with a guy* and not *Are you okay?* What third grader is doing anything with a guy and being okay? She must not have known how to approach such a taboo, uncomfortable subject, with secondhand information to boot. She was a good person, a good teacher, but as a result of her botched attempt at helping me I became even more silent. As for the girl I had told, I didn't really talk to her after that. We were never close friends anyway.

The abuse finally ended when I ended it. I said to him, *You have to stop doing this.* I was getting older and could make the decision whether or not I wanted to visit Dad at Lee Roy's house.

When enough time had passed to look back, I felt so angry at everyone for letting it all happen, for not seeing to it that I was protected. When I get upset, I have to talk about it. I talked about it with Akasha. *You think you were the only one?* she scoffed. But of course not. I never saw anything happen to my sister, and she has never told me about it in detail. I just know that we have this thing in common with who knows how many other females in our family. I thought that I was getting abused and Akasha wasn't, and it was because I was fat and Akasha was not. She was a tow-headed, cotton-headed blonde, delicate, thin, and girly. Protected, I thought, by this conventional prettiness. Safe and skinny. But it wasn't true.

Years later, in the middle of the woods in Washington, Gossip's guitarist Nathan Howdeshell and I were working late on a sad little somber song about secrets in the dark: "Holy Water." From front to finish it was written and recorded in a matter of minutes. When I emerged from my vocal-booth time capsule it was very late. There was a message from my dad telling me Lee Roy had died. *Just thought you should know.*

I tried to look out for the other kids. I tried really hard to make sure my little cousins were taken care of. I saved pennies for the oldest one so she could watch them collect in a jar and then I'd slide them into wrappers when I had enough. I liked the weight of the rolls in my palm, the order of the change snug inside the paper. It felt like I was really giving her something she could use—giving her a little say. But what she really needed was the same thing her brother needed, and what I needed—help—and there was no one around who had any.

10

Like I've told you, Arkansas is a good ten years behind the times, so basically the whole country was well aware of grunge when I started getting my first, excited understanding of the phenomenon. While the rest of the country was in head-to-toe flannel, I was wearing my hair higher than my Aunt Jannie's blood sugar levels. Things take a while to get to places like Judsonia, and then they take a while to leave. It was hard for me to abandon my big hair, no matter how cool Alanis Morissette was, or how cozy flannel could be. I lived to rat my hair, and I was good at it. Really good at it.

If I had a perm and bangs you can be sure I had the best curls, the tallest bangs. I knew how to do it. I was so good at doing hair that kids who wouldn't look at me twice in the hall were risking major injury to their reputations by asking me to come to their houses and give them their prom updos. I could do anything with hair, so I had to find a way to fit my talents into my new grunge lifestyle. Out of all the friends I was making in high school—and there weren't that many—I became the best at the Kool-Aid dye job. I made up my own personal technique, which was to mix two packets of Kool-Aid with a creamy dollop of Noxzema—just about the size of a dime or a quarter—and let it sit on my head for hours, so my hair color was really bright. I still love the smell of Noxzema, how it sears your nose with that eucalyptus stink.

My Kool-Aid pink hair and Converse weren't fooling anyone, though; I was still anything but cool, but I didn't mind. In my own grassroots movement at my high school I orchestrated a hostile nerd takeover. When it came time to vote for Accolades— the smarmy who's who of the school: who's cutest, funniest, smartest—I persuaded the entire school to vote for my friends, the nerds. I campaigned on behalf of dorks and skanks, teenage moms, sluts, and weirdos, and it worked. We won everything. I was a lucky weirdo at my school, blessed with a total obliviousness to whether people liked me. If you care what the right people—your friends—think of you, you're free to do anything, and I didn't give a shit how my classmates regarded me. If you weren't my friend, I didn't care. Not getting invited to a party is worth it; that missing invitation can say important things about who you are and what you value. I didn't get beat up, and that gave me room to be outrageous without fear of serious consequence. I made people laugh. I was that fat kid who beat people to the punch, who survived by being funny. And everyone likes a funny person. Everyone likes to laugh.

The crowning glory of the nerd takeover I'd orchestrated at school was successfully getting myself elected to represent my class at Fall Festival. Fall Festival is just a tiny little beauty pageant, but in Judsonia it's a big deal, a time-honored tradition, a fund-raiser for the high school. Everyone wanted to be in Fall Festival, from the popular girls to regular ones.

All the people nominated for Fall Festival had to leave the classroom. All the popular girls—as popular as you can be in a place that isn't very populated—and Mary Beth Ditto. This kid Trevarar made a noise and jerked around in his desk. *That's all we need, a skank representing our class!* And that year a skank *did* represent our class. I got elected to Fall Festival because all the nerds liked me and there are more nerds than non-nerds. I was the one nerdy fat girl, the weirdo, the punk Riot Grrrl, the Kool-Aid-headed funny girl up there on the stage with all the popular girls. All of those girls who were the exact opposite of me.

I had a lot of friends and, though we might not have been the A crowd, we were definitely the most fun. Tonya was my oldest and closest friend—oldest in the sense that she flunked a couple of grades and had been held back more than once. Tonya was cool. She ordered her clothes from the Delia's catalog. I was so horribly jealous; she had the cutest T-shirts and baby-doll dresses. It was so simple for her; she just picked her look right off of the catalog page. She loved Sonic Youth so much I just couldn't bring myself to listen to them for years. She could have Sonic Youth.

My fashion evolution went like this: right before I found punk, I wanted to look like Mary Tyler Moore from *The Dick Van Dyke Show*. I wanted to look like Janis Joplin, Patty Duke, and Mama Cass, all rolled into one girl. Never mind that all those women were rocking different looks to go with their different genres and scenes; to me it was all the '60s, it was all the same, and I liked all of it.

I had three obstacles in my way when it came to clothes: money (didn't have it), size (I was fat), and style (there was none in Arkansas). Then, something came to my rescue: old reliable resourcefulness. If I wanted something cool, I had to sew it myself. My mom and I would make patterns by tracing clothes that fit me onto newspaper pages. Almost every special piece I wore was either made by me or for me. In some ways, that still rings true.

I was desperate for subculture. I took it any way I could get it. I had access to old TV shows, old magazines, and old music. I was infatuated with the stories of my mother's childhood friend

Dan—who, like me, is an escapee of White County. Even though I didn't know him, he inspired me. I wanted to be just like him. When he was a kid he was arrested for spray painting stop signs. He simply added the word WAR, so when drivers in oncoming traffic read it, they read STOP WAR. By the time the '80s rolled around Dan was long gone and making a living off of his art in Seattle at a time when to most people, "Washington" meant the nation's capital. Thus began my fixation on the Pacific Northwest.

At the beginning of junior high a girl who had been on my periphery became one of my most important friends. She was funny and laughed at everything. Crystal and I had a lot of fun together. Funny people are always my favorites. Somewhere in my box of pictures is one of us together at school, dressed exactly alike. We owned matching R.E.M. T-shirts. Together we redecorated her room. We listened to Nirvana's *Incesticide* on cassette. We played it on repeat. Nirvana was our eighth-grade soundtrack. We spent days covering her pink ballerina wallpaper with big, psychedelic swirls of sidewalk chalk and sprayed the whole thing down with shellac so it would stay. We had so much fun together and stayed close for two summers, but as junior high was ending, Crystal met a boy, and eventually so did I.

I'd seen Anthony around my whole life, but we officially met on the school bus. I'd had my eye on him since junior high. He was noticeable in his Nirvana T-shirt. Nobody else had one of those, not even me. I thought Anthony was pretty cool. He was wearing a pair of really sad combat boots, and his hair was long. By the time we started dating, Anthony still had his Nirvana shirt, faded and better looking, and he still had the tragic combat boots with the frayed laces, but his tangle of long, cool hair was chopped off. His dad had given him an ultimatum: you can have long hair, or you can have a car. In Judsonia, the choice was easy. Wear your hair in a hairdo that gets you beat up and not have the wheels to speed yourself away from your tormentors, or cut your mop and have freedom of movement.

One day I finally got up the courage to uncoolly ask if Anthony liked punk. He was so sweet and shy that he didn't even speak, he just nodded yes. I asked him to a show and he nodded yes again. He finally gave me his phone number. I tried to play it cool, but I was stressed because I didn't have a phone number to give him—I didn't even know where I'd be sleeping that night.

One week later we were boyfriend-girlfriend and we stayed coupled up like that for three whole years. After school I would walk a mile to the pay phone to call him. If he wasn't there it would be so depressing. It was even worse if he was in the bathroom, taking a shower. Phone calls cost a dime. If I had two dimes I could hang around for a minute and try again, but I often had only a single dime.

Anthony and I had a really sweet relationship. I told him about my uncle, and that I couldn't remember ever being a virgin. Anthony was a feminist boy, compassionate and patient with me. He listened to a lot of the same music I did and we shared mix tapes. We had endless conversations about music, and with our information exchange, both of our music libraries doubled. He played guitar and I liked to sing, and since we had so many great influences, we decided to start the world's shittiest band, Little Miss Muffet. Anthony named it.

Little Miss Muffet was so silly. We had one song called "Ziggy Nut." I still don't know what it was about. Our drummer, Joey Story, was only thirteen years old. He was kind of a surly kid, and he had a real sweet mom who let us practice in her living room.

Little Miss Muffet had our first show at this place called Hastings. It didn't make any sense for us to be part of that show, but we were. Joey had an older brother named Dean, who was in a band called Room Fullove Thirteen. They sounded like Third Eye Blind or Blink-182, or something awful like that. They had fancy banners announcing their band. I felt like Room Fullove Thirteen was just mocking us, all the time, because we were the shittiest band with the shittiest equipment, and you could tell they thought they were really going somewhere. They would take their equipment around in a trailer, while we showed up in our car with a busted-ass Peavey amp. Joey and Dean's father, Mr. Story, was deep in the throes of a midlife crisis. He'd left Mrs. Story, bought a super-fancy car, and was fake-managing Room Fullove Thirteen. It was like something you'd see on TV, like a bad reality show that makes you cringe because the people all think they're really going somewhere but you, the viewer, understand they're going nowhere fast.

We played a couple of shows together. It made me realize that even within the "us" there is a "them." Like, Room Fullove Thirteen were sort of weird for Arkansas, but next to nerds like me and Anthony, they were normal. They, like everyone else, didn't know what to make of us.

There was Room Fullove Thirteen, Little Miss Muffet, and Nathan's band, Mrs. Garrett, which is how I first learned of the whole Nathan phenomenon. Nathan had a tape distro, where he copied the shitty demo tapes of various bands and sold them to people via mail order, or at his shows. He put out a tape of Little Miss Muffet without even asking us! Nathan was so exciting and different, but he was only one of the cool new people I was meeting.

Around that time, my gay feelings were becoming unavoidable. I didn't have any doubts about how I felt. I had two options: coming out and not knowing what the future held, or staying in and becoming a typical Judsonia woman. In my desperation, I wanted an easy out, and I figured that a baby would be a certain way to avoid the looming eternity of hellfire and brimstone I was sure was in store for me. Plus, so many other girls were having babies that it seemed normal. I started begging Anthony to knock me up. It is ironic that after spending so much time worrying I'd wind up pregnant, now that I was trying to make it happen, it just wouldn't. It helped that Anthony flat-out refused—no sperm, no baby. I think it must have been a real God spell that my mother put on me, if you want to know the truth. She never wanted us to wind up like her, saddled with so many babies, even as she kept having them. She wanted a different life for me, and she used her strange witchy ways to give me this one kind of protection, and it worked. Anthony didn't knock me up, and I stayed gay inside; my secret.

Meanwhile, we were doing shows with Room Fullove Thirteen because there just weren't that many bands to ask to play. The same small group of people were in all the bands, mixing around into different combinations. Little Miss Muffet and Room Fullove Thirteen, Mrs. Garrett, and Space Kadets, who were also called Boy Pussy USA. Not to forget my future friends Jeri Beard and Kathy Mendonca's band, Poopoo Icee. They had a second band, the Velvet 45s. And there were the Puget Sounds and the Hips. Every day was a different band, almost. Someone would get inspired by a new cool band name and voilà, a fresh ensemble would debut. It was so exciting, this whole music thing, and up until then everything in Arkansas had been so incredibly boring.

It was Nathan who brought the whole scene together. Nathan is truly a magical person. He's always been able to make things happen; he's never bored. If he notices something being boring he fixes it really easily, and I felt that's what he did with his hometown, Searcy.

Searcy was still Arkansas, but it was a little bigger, a little cooler, with more pipelines to the outside world. Nathan was too cool. He wasn't wearing baggy jeans and a wallet chain, he was watching John Waters films and wearing a polyester suit. Really, really cool.

Our "audiences" were very small. Mostly we just played for each other, unless Room Fullove Thirteen were on the bill. They all had girlfriends who would stand at the front of the stage and sway and coo at them the whole time, and of course their ever-present manager-dad would be around. Once Mom came to listen to me sing. She was really into Little Miss Muffet and really sweet about my voice. She hadn't gotten to go to many of my things when I was a kid, choir and whatnot, so she tried to make up for it during my teen years.

Just because I was trying my hand at singing for bands didn't mean I'd abandoned the choir. I was such a choir nerd I'd been voted choir president! Bet you didn't even know such a position existed. I'd shamelessly campaigned for the slot, and I'd gotten it, because in spite of everything I was well liked. I had a *Why not?* attitude about things that freed me up to go after stuff a more hesitant nerd—or even worse, a more popular kid—might avoid.

11

As hard as it was to scrounge for music, desperately trying to hunt down what kids in other cities had easy access to, there was something special about that time. Each discovery was a treasure that could save your life, that made you more understandable to yourself. Every song was a message in a bottle cast into the ocean by someone just like you, in another land, who was waiting for you to join her, saying, *You'll make it! You'll make it!* I'm glad I came of age during that weird window before kids could download music on the Internet.

When Jennifer came into my life it really changed everything. I met my chosen family through Jennifer. She introduced me to my bandmates and best friends: her boyfriend, Jeri, and Kathy and Nathan. Jennifer was the daughter of Jo Ann, the lady who had introduced my mother to Tom. Jennifer had been living with her dad in Monroe, Louisiana, but then her dad got remarried and Jennifer couldn't find her place in that family, so she came to Arkansas to stay with her mom. I could already relate to this girl skipping across state lines, trying to figure out where her home was. Monroe wasn't the coolest place to be stuck, but at least they had MTV. Judsonia had banned the station in the '80s, so seeing music videos there was practically impossible. Jennifer came prepared. Before she left Louisiana she recorded a whole bunch of videos off MTV—Hole, Veruca Salt, Nine Inch Nails, Nirvana, Alanis Morissette. We'd watch them over and over: Trent Reznor shirtless, Veruca Salt's kittens, French bulldogs, and dolls, Nirvana's apocalyptic high school cheerleaders in their black Converse. Jennifer showed me her videos and I showed her what I'd scrounged here and there. She was the answer to my prayers. Suddenly, I felt completely understood. She bridged the gap from choir girl to youth movement. I owe life as I know it to our brief but fulfilling friendship.

Everything about my meeting Jennifer was fated. We didn't go to school together, and there was really no reason our paths should ever have crossed. Jennifer came to my mother's house with her mom one night—a night that I happened to be there.

Jennifer was a little freaked out from landing in Arkansas. Monroe was a fascinating metropolis compared to Morning Sun, the town she was living in. Morning Sun has since been swallowed up by Searcy, so it's a little more urban, but not much, and not then. It was amazing to have this girl about my age, just a year older, show up at my house in the middle of nowhere, Arkansas, liking the same kind of music I liked. Jennifer was wearing a really cool pair of pants that were super baggy. I wanted pants like that so bad but had no idea where to get them. In my town, to get Converse you had to ask a store to order them for you special, and for a bondage belt—a leather belt decorated with shiny silver loops—you had to go into a straight-up sex shop.

Jennifer came around at the moment when I was growing out of grunge and getting more into Riot Grrrl. Happening right alongside grunge, rising up and out of that same Pacific Northwest music scene that was spitting out Nirvana and the other boy bands, was a rebellious, smart, tough, and unabashedly female—

even feminine—movement being tagged Riot Grrrl. Riot Grrrl took the second-wave feminist adage "The personal is political" and brought it home to young women in the grunge and punk scenes. Think it's sort of weird that all the bands are men, that grunge and punk boys are just as shitty to girls as a room full of frat boys? Riot Grrrl addressed it. Think it's just a coincidence that pretty much every girl you have ever met has sustained some sort of sexual trauma? Riot Grrrl called the bullshit: it's called misogyny, it's a systemic cultural problem, it affects punk scenes, and it is political. The way girls are taught to hate their bodies unless they are skinny, inspiring self-loathing, self-hate, disordered eating? It's political. Riot Grrrl said so. Homophobia is political, racism is political, and here was a revolution centered around music that affirmed girls, girlishness, females, and feminism, overtly, with all the fuck-you of punk rock. With grunge on one side of me and Riot Grrrl on the other, I finally felt like there was something out there in the larger world that maybe could catch me when and if I ever jumped out of this life in Arkansas.

At age twelve, I had begun identifying as a feminist. It was sometimes very confusing to be a feminist who loves a campy Greta Garbo brow and enjoys drawing on a Madonna mole. Discovering Riot Grrrl gave me insight into the beauty myth—my lipstick could be an inch thick and my hair could be a mile high, and my identity as a feminist was intact. So did I put my hairspray down? No. I moved my rattail comb from the front of my head to the back and bouffanted my hair. Just like the Huggy Bear song.

Riot Grrrl kept a magpie aesthetic, nicking styles from punk subcultures, from grunge and goth. It detested capitalism and so it was thrifted, secondhand, or you made it yourself. Riot Grrrl lifted its ban on capitalism long enough to slink into a mall and emerge with a head full of brightly colored plastic baby barrettes and Hello Kitty paraphernalia. It inverted the definitions of nerdy and cool.

Trapped in Arkansas, I dreamed of my soul sisters in Washington State. It was hard out there to really stay on top of what was happening everywhere else, but by the time I caught on, Riot Grrrl had already shown up in *Time* magazine, and in the pages of *Sassy*. It was a real movement, big enough to send its ripples all the way to Judsonia. Never mind that Riot Grrrl was fading out in the places where it had begun; in Arkansas it was only beginning to reach us. It was still new, exotic, empowering, exciting. We couldn't afford *Sassy*, so we didn't have the latest info about trends the rest of the nation was experiencing, but that didn't make us any less excited about it.

Jennifer and I would stay up late singing Counting Crows songs into a tape recorder and making up our own songs too. I loved to sing, I loved to take the thoughts in my mind and braid them into a melody. It felt good to push the sound out into the air with my body. Singing was simple and powerful at once. We would cover songs we liked, making them sound terrible, playing them back on the warbly, scratchy tape player, cracking up.

In high school I had an intense awakening. I'd been trying to make sense out of so much chaos for so long and it exploded. I looked around and I saw insanity, and I knew that there was something wrong but it wasn't me, so I wasn't going to act like I was anything less than excellent. It was a shaky conviction, but it was inside me. And I had the music to back me up. I had these movements— Riot Grrrl, grunge—happening in other places, cheering me on, wanting me to win, to triumph over the rapists and the ignorant racists and the mundane and the boring. There was a big life out there and I was starting to feel it. If I could just survive Arkansas, I'd maybe be able to get to it.

I started fighting back against what I saw. I started standing up to my teachers about things like abortion and racism and going against the grain by being one of the only girls who dared to take shop class instead of home economics. I was already cooking and cleaning and sewing at home—why would I want to come to school and do that?

The topics I selected for my speech class really summed up my place within that school. I was actually liked by a lot of the teachers, in spite of how provocative I'd become. In Speech I did two final projects. One was on how to apply makeup, and the other was on violence against women around the world and how we still accept it every single day.

Senior year we were all required to take a class called Family Dynamics. You had to take it, everyone did. We were taught . . . family dynamics. STDs, birth control. By then we were all seventeen or eighteen years old. Some of us were nineteen or twenty: the flunkies. We were sitting at these tables taking tests with questions like "Are you pro-choice, yes or no?" Students graded one another's papers, so everyone knew one another's business. When we were through, the teacher asked the class, *Who said they are pro-choice?* Me and Tonya were the only ones who checked yes on that question. Even though half the girls in the class had been pregnant and half of those girls had probably had actual abortions. A third of the class had kids already, and half of those moms had had abortions as well. The truth was that girls were either having babies or having abortions. In Family Dynamics we were being taught how to avoid STDs and . . . how to pick out an engagement ring! Most of our parents didn't even have engagement rings because we were so fucking poor. Most of us were getting free lunch at school each day.

Family Dynamics was insane, absurd, and offensive, but we took it seriously. We had to. The woman teaching us was the same woman who had taught our parents that shit, and it was about respect and tradition, and so we did our best to pass the test given on the difference between a princess-cut and a square-cut diamond. Those were the skills we were taught.

· · ·

Meanwhile, my classmates' gaydar was going off when I walked down the halls at school. *Are you a dyke?* Maybe it was my short, short hair. Or maybe it was that I'm actually a dyke. Either way, it's uncomfortable to have people seeing your insides before you're ready to show them. It made me so mad. It wasn't like it is today. Things have gotten better for queers even in places like Arkansas. Now my little sister roams the halls at that same high school bragging about what a flaming bisexual she is. But I didn't feel that cocky. All I had to do was think about what happened to Mr. Skate at Fun Time Skate Land and I wanted to crawl away and hide my queerness under a pile of babies.

Fun Time Skate Land was a roller rink in Judsonia. There was speculation that Mr. Skate was gay. He was very effeminate, round and balding, a soft bear. He was also a nice guy and all the kids really liked him. And we loved Fun Time Skate Land. The DJ booth was on the edge of the rink, and if you skated up to make a request you'd cause the needle to jump on the vinyl and the DJ would give you a dirty look. You could buy fat dill pickles from a big pickle jar. The one year I remember having a birthday party, my tenth, I had it at Fun Time Skate Land, and it was the best birthday I've ever had in my life. It was great. But it got shut down in the early '90s because Mr. Skate had allegedly been out cruising and got busted.

For those of you who don't know, cruising is a beloved pastime of lots of gay men: you go out into some area, like a park or a bathroom, and you meet up with other guys who want to have sex, and then you have sex. It happens in big cities and it happens in small towns. It happens in the Macy's men's bathrooms in San Francisco and the Fenway Victory Gardens in Boston and in too many truck stops to list all across the United States. Mr. Skate was allegedly cruising at Berryhill Park, a place that gets all lit up with Christmas lights. Unbeknownst to the locals ignorant of homosexual culture, it was where a guy could hang out and meet another guy for sex. Mr. Skate got busted by a cop there.

At that time, Judsonia wasn't the only place in the United States that would have gladly persecuted a grown man for having an alternative lifestyle, but if you think about what was going on in 1991 in places like San Francisco and Chicago and D.C. and Olympia, Washington, where Riot Grrrl and homocore punk were brewing, and how that attitude impacted the mainstream, now we live in its aftermath, and things are a little different. All across the country, sending inspiration even into deep Arkansas, the efforts of people who cared about building a better world—one with more acceptance, more outrage toward violence—landed in the minds of real people, and things changed. It was our version of the sixties "revolution"—a loose group of young people who were rejecting the nihilist fashion-punk of the eighties and trying to build punk into a movement that included women, queers, and community values. The very idea that women should be allowed to play guitars and take the mic was in a lot of ways a revelation at the time; prioritizing inclusiveness in musical scenes was shocking because it reverberated outward into an insistence on inclusiveness as a value in life. We were just writing political sentiments into songs, or trying to get our zines into the world, and some people were creating spaces where girls could come and talk, for the first time, about violence that had been done to them. There were just small things, but they added up. It was like an excellent virus, everyone fighting to change their little part of the world and it all coming together like a puzzle.

12

It was at the start of the school day. I still had sleep crusting in my eyeliner—I had to wake up so early to haul myself all the way from Georgetown—when someone told me about Dean.

This girl grabbed me. *Did you hear? Dean got arrested for rape.* Was I so sleepy that I wasn't hearing things right? *What?*

Dean got arrested. For rape. She was talking about my cousin.

The thing was, sexual abuse in my family went back so far, tracing it was impossible. Who knows what might have happened to Dean? If it was hard for girls to talk about their abuse, how much harder was it for a boy? Did something horrible happen to Dean to make him into that type of monster? Or maybe it was something else entirely. What made Uncle Lee Roy the sort of monster he was? My head hurt just thinking about all of it.

Two days later it was announced that Dean was being prosecuted for the rape of my two younger cousins, and everything suddenly made sense. The things that they had tried to tell me, that I hadn't understood. With a few years under my belt, and a deeper understanding of feminism, I was able to put two and two together. My sweet little cousin and the gold ring. Mom put that together, how Dean must have used the jewelry as a bribe to convince my cousin to do things with him. I was reeling with the severity of it. Laws had been broken. This stuff wasn't actually supposed to be happening. My little cousins were taken away from Aunt Jannie's, but they were sent back to their horrible mother. I truly don't know where they'd have been better off.

Mom asked me if I'd ever noticed anything funny at Aunt Jannie's. Funny? With Aunt Jannie herself setting the standard for normal behavior, what would it take for something to stand out?

13

Jeri won't kiss me, Jennifer said, nervously, one day.

He's gay, I thought. I heard it from the same inner voice that told me *I'm gay* all the time—reverberating, ricocheting, resisting all my efforts to shut it up. This Jeri person had to be gay. He had to be! Boys started doing it with girls so young in Judsonia, and it's all they ever did. It was unthinkable that a teenage boy with a proper girlfriend wouldn't kiss her! If things were normal Jennifer would have had a couple of pregnancy scares by now, or a couple of abortions, maybe an actual kid toddling around. Gay, gay gay, gay gay. The word pulsed in my head, but I didn't say it to Jennifer. It would break her heart and freak her out, and who knew, anyway? Maybe I was wrong. But I knew I wasn't! *What else can I say?* Kurt Cobain says. *Everyone is gay.*

I was tremendously excited about this Jeri person and his probable gayness. I couldn't wait to meet him. I didn't want to act too eager, because I didn't want Jennifer to get the wrong idea and think I was after her boyfriend. I mean, I was—just not like that. I was after another gay person to help quell the fears that I was going to hell. I was scared of God. It's hard to grow up in Arkansas and not be! The folks who want you to be spooked by their idea of God put a lot of time and money into their cause. There are big signs all over Arkansas saying, WHAT WILL YOU DO WHEN THE END COMES? and GOD HAS HIS EYES ON YOU! You see them when you're out in the car. We'd drive past them in the school bus, or when we were heading back to Georgetown with my dad. *God has his eyes on you.* Oh, great. Then he knew I was queer and, according to the jabbering of folks I knew, the ones who professed to really know God's opinion on things like homosexuality, I was going to be spending eternity in a lake of fire. I don't know, none of it made sense, but I was scared anyway. I didn't want anything bad to happen to me, and I didn't want God to hate me.

The night I finally met Jeri almost never happened. Jennifer didn't want to go to the seedy game room where all her friends were getting together. She twirled her stringy, perfectly grunge hair around her fingers and moped about it, but she finally agreed.

We met up with everyone at the depressing game room and de-camped for Jeri's house. I never cared what anyone thought about me until that night. I was half in myself and half too terrified to be there. I felt awkward and excited. I knew that these were the cool-est people I had ever met. I wanted them to like me. Really, really bad! I worked hard to stay composed but not too cool—I wanted them to know I liked them, but not too much. My head spun with it all. There was Jeri, Jennifer's maybe-secretly-gay boyfriend. There was Nathan, who I'd heard all about, but had never spoken to. There was Kathy, a city kid: very badass. Kathy lived in Searcy, a true city by any kind of local standard. Every weekend your mom would say, *I'm going to town,* by which she'd mean Searcy. My mom still says it. I loved going into town, and Kathy lived there!

The centerpiece of Jeri's messy bedroom was his computer. Jeri was a crazy computer whiz. He still is. He had a computer pro-gram that let you take a picture of someone's face and morph it into grotesque, hilarious images. These kids didn't know me at all;

they were being so rude to me! Taking my picture and morphing it into a monster, making fun of me. They intimidated the shit out of me. They passed around rumpled zines from Jeri's collection. I had never heard of zines, which were little magazines made by kids like us, chock full of whatever a person happened to be interested in, his drawings and writings, interviews he'd managed to score with bands he loved. Scrawled in ink or pounded out on a typewriter, then Xeroxed somehow into a little booklet and sent out into the world. People traded zines with one another, but if you were like us, living in Arkansas, you found zines the same way you found music and fashion: through mail order. Looking through Jeri's zine collection, the fullness of Riot Grrrl philosophy and aesthetics overwhelmed me. It was a treasure chest of everything I cared about; my dreams were so in line with the dreams of all these strangers who had gotten them on paper and sent them out into the world. I could have sat there all night with my face in Jeri's collection, but I wanted my new friends to think I was used to this kind of stuff.

Jeri had record players and bunches of records, and he played DJ as everyone talked, dropping names of bands I hadn't heard of, laughing at jokes I couldn't know were funny but somehow completely understood.

These kids were really creative; all of them drew. They were the coolest. They were products of Christian Arkansas who had recently escaped from the Christian youth groups that so many adolescents get shuffled into. They were getting old enough to think for themselves, and they were shuffling on out. Still, the Christian organization had left its mark on them. They were weirdly antisex. Everyone was creeped out by fornication, and it struck me as a strangely punk rock attitude. If punk is about being against the dominant culture, being antisex was way punk, because the culture that had been dominating me my whole life was wildly, inappropriately, abusively sexual. My new, unfriendly friends also refrained from drinking, taking drugs, or smoking. I hid my cigarettes from them. I kept my pot smoking secret too, since they thought marijuana was so uncool. Before, I had never cared what anyone thought about my habits. Now all I wanted was their approval. I laughed at all their jokes. The things that came out of their mouths were ungodly! The jokes weren't about fags, or black people, or at the expense of a girl. Their humor was avant-garde nonsense. It was a defining moment: for the first time, I got the joke! Jeri laughed at me for being such a dork, cracking up hysterically at their weirdo quips and observations. Nathan scoffed at my enthusiasm, and Kathy just regarded me silently. I was one of them.

Kathy was the first feminist I had ever met. Whatever I'd gleaned about feminism via Riot Grrrl now came into sharp focus in the form of the girl standing in front of me. I remember hearing the word "feminist" when I was just a kid—eleven years old— and identifying with it even then, though in a Feminism 101/ Gloria Steinem/Girl Power way, too young to comprehend anything deeper. Kathy seemed to understand the detailed picture of feminism, though it was hard to get her to talk about what she knew because she was so crazy quiet. In a gang of loudmouths, all of us hollering and laughing all the time, Kathy was remarkable for her silence. She didn't feel like she had to talk to anyone. She just hung around with all her hair in her face, projecting cool, radical wisdom. When she did speak, you could hear how she spoke without a Southern accent. *You're so quiet!* I'd exclaim, and she'd sink deeper into her long, glossy bangs. I didn't know she hated that I did that, the way shy people always hate it when you make a fuss out of their shyness. I just wanted to interact with her so badly and she was so aloof.

Kathy was the first girl I ever knew I had a crush on. I had a crush. On a girl. I was delighted by it, really. I just hung around, waiting for her to speak, enchanted by her quiet, so different from me. She shrugged. *If I don't have anything to say, I don't say it.* Well, I'm just the opposite. If I don't have anything to say, I'm going to say everything. Kathy was such a mystery to me. I thought she was the best thing I'd ever seen, and I still feel that way about her. She was always wearing leopard-print tights. We had to work so hard for what we had. If you were lucky you could find something good to wear at the Goodwill or Wal-Mart, but that was it. God knows how many paychecks it took Kathy to save up and order her cool leopard leggings through the mail. Those tights were her trademark. So was her voice, the way she talked like a Riot Grrrl, or like a Valley Girl, like she came from a faraway state that had an ocean and a lot of people having all sorts of conversations in their super-cool voices.

Jeri and Nathan sort of talked like that too, like they were torn, wanting to ditch their native accents but scared of sounding phony. I thought my own voice sounded dumb, lumbering, beside Kathy's. I tried to copy her, but it didn't work out for me. My accent is seared onto my voice same as my fingerprints are grooved into my thumbs.

Kathy lived with her mother, who was a good, sweet Christian lady who had psychological problems that had put her through hell in the '70s. Her inappropriateness was sporadic and jarring, like how she taught Kathy to call her vagina her pussy, not her privates like other little girls. It must have been a shock to hear the P-word coming out of the innocent mouth of a tiny girl. No wonder Kathy didn't talk much.

Nathan's band, Mrs. Garrett, was named after the shrill, bouffanted den mother from the '80s TV show *The Facts of Life*. He had a second band, with Jeri, first called Space Kadet, then Boy Pussy USA—Boy Pussy for short. Their flyers were hand-drawn cartoons of the band members in dresses with pieces of food flying out of their mouths. They drew big bouffant hairdos onto their cartoon heads. God, I wanted them to like me so bad! I had never been so on edge.

Under their influence, my fashion slowly improved. We were so far removed from everything—punk, Riot Grrrl—that our expression of the culture had its own special Arkansas spin. We weren't exactly punk rock, though we tried. I had a new Mr. Potato Head ringer T, replacing the Pearl Jam T-shirt I'd been living in. I wore wacky shoes and purple fingernail polish and baby barrettes in my hair.

I wanted to get my nose pierced so badly! In bigger cities, piercing boutiques had sprung up. You could buy fancy jewelry made especially for noses or eyebrows or belly buttons there. Not in Judsonia. I went to the Town and Country Plaza, where a hair salon next to the JCPenney would pierce your ears for you. I went inside and asked the lady if she'd do my nose. *Your what?* She looked at me like I was crazy, but she took the metal piercer and angled it up inside my nose. I'm sure there is some sanitary law against that. The piercing gun was bulky and my nostril was too small. Since she couldn't get the angle right, my nose was pierced on a slant, but it was pierced, and it looked cool.

I looked way better, more worthy of the company of my new friends. Because slowly, that's who they were becoming—my friends.

It took more than a nose ring for Nathan to warm up to me, though. Nathan had single-handedly created a punk scene in our shitty small town. He'd even gotten Dub Narcotic Sound System to come and play. Nathan put on shows in the Legion Hut; they only charged twenty-four dollars to rent the place. Nathan was a hero. Part Native American, he has hair that is naturally coal black—the color everyone stained their necks trying to get from a box. His hair always looked cool. He's worn thick Buddy Holly glasses for as long as I've known him. He was so committed to his look that he wore three-piece polyester suits and a ten-pound dog chain around his neck, even during the brutal Arkansas summer. The school administration eventually banned Nathan's chains; unfortunately for them, there was no banning polyester. Nathan was a distraction in the classroom. He just sat there like a big "Fuck you, Arkansas" and got his ass kicked by jocks all the time for it. He got fag-bashed, the prevailing wisdom being that any guy who looked weird must be a fag. But Nathan wasn't gay. *Just taking one for the team,* he'd say philosophically. Assholes would spit their food at him in the cafeteria, and he'd pick it up and eat it. Such style! I never knew anyone who got beat up more than Nathan. He was so suspicious of me, it set me on edge. Our tiny punk scene was a bit of a boy's club, and I was a girl—a fat, loud, nerdy, obnoxious girl.

The first time I went to Nathan's I was chased off the land by a shotgun. Nathan's dad, Eddie, loved guns. He chased me off the land, wasted, in a golf cart, because I'd been shooting bottle rockets into their barn. *I'll shoot your ass!* Nathan actually gets a lot of his character from his dad.

Nathan was one of two kids. His mom ran off. She was awful. She would meet Nathan at the end of the long road that led to his house and take his lunch money for drugs. She'd leave for weeks at a time before leaving for good. She would call his younger sister and promise she was coming home for Christmas, and the sister would wrap up a bunch of presents. There was a stockpile of gifts collecting dust in a closet at Nathan's for this woman who never came through. It was a familiar scene to me because I'd seen the same thing happen with the mother of the three A's. She'd talk a big game about coming to see my cousins, but then she'd never show up, or she'd show up late on a school night a week later. Knowing that kind of stuff about Nathan made me feel closer to him.

What bands do you know? Nathan asked me one day, like it was a quiz. I was sure there were right answers and wrong answers, but I only knew the bands I knew, so I answered honestly. *Melanie. Mama Cass.* Nathan ignored me. I was way into Missy Elliott. But I loved Raoul and Skinned Teen and Sleater-Kinney too. I still love Sleater-Kinney. *Call the Doctor* stands the test of time; it's one of the best albums ever made.

Nathan had a musician's pride in his knowledge and appreciation of all sorts of music, not just punk. One night at Jeri's he was talking about blues records, and I leapt at the chance to be impressive. I loved the blues! *I love Billie Holiday,* I chimed in. Nathan looked over at me.

Yeah, I like him too.

Come again?

Billie Holiday, I like him too, he repeated.

Yep, I croaked. *Billie Holiday . . . He's excellent.*

Nathan just wanted to know everything. I knew something about music that he didn't; I had seen his cool façade crack and caught a glimpse of another insecure teen. It helped me relax. They were all just nerds on the inside too. Of course Nathan was guarded, getting his ass kicked all over town. He had finally found his group of people and it was hard to let a new one in.

It was eventually Jeri who got the others to warm up to me. Jeri's a redhead, and, when we were teens, his hair was long and filthy. Jeri wore Nintendo controllers around his neck like jewelry; he was obsessed with *Mortal Kombat.* He'd cut the legs off his pants and pin them to the sleeves of his T-shirts with safety pins. He cut up his socks and wore them as arm warmers. He wore Dickies shirts that he wrote all over with Sharpies. The shirts said things like REJECT ALL AMERICAN. At one point he'd broken both his wrists and was walking around with a pair of casts tagged up in the most hilarious shit. He was a brilliant techie and had been busted when he was fifteen years old for hacking into the phone company and stealing long-distance for a year.

I knew from the moment I met Jeri that he was gay. I could tell, and I wanted him to know that I could tell, and to tell him it was okay with me because I was gay too. One night at the county fair, walking the midway with all the crazy lights flashing, I whispered in Jeri's ear (please feel free to laugh at this), *I'm a flaming bisexual!* Bisexuality seemed cool. I could have these gay insides but still keep my boyfriend, Anthony. Maybe there'd still be a way to get pregnant and have babies and the gay part would fade away.

Oh, that's cool, Jeri said. Jennifer was walking beside him, bored, but we hardly noticed her. The truth was, the four of us were growing very close, and my friendship with Jennifer started to go by the wayside. Jeri and I were especially tight and had deep conversations, the kind he couldn't have with Nathan, who was all jokes and music. Jeri was sensitive behind his constant goofing; he wanted friendships that could get deep and serious too—because life was pretty much always absurd, but it wasn't always funny.

I was hanging out at Jeri's house one afternoon, watching some shitty talk show. The topic that day was "Fat People Who Dress Too Sexy for Their Size." Those shows were always on, and I'd seen them before, watched them at my mother's home, slumped on the couch next to her. *Oh, slap the cookie out of my hand if I ever get that big,* she'd say. In Jeri's bedroom, sloshing around on his waterbed, I looked at the television and said, *Oh my god, look at those women.*

Who cares? Jeri, who is fat, said. *What makes somebody "too fat"? Why does it have to be like that?*

Jeri had been reading Nomy Lamm's fat-positive zine *I'm So Fucking Beautiful*. Those zines were creating a feminist subculture, and their ideas trickled down to me, through Jeri, and I eventually started using the word "fat" positively. After that, I started to realize just how much my body image had been affecting my life. I never felt like a real singer. Real singers were small and had sweet, soft voices and sounded like the girls from the Murmurs, or else they had shrill punk rock crazy voices like a cheerleader turned inside out, like Kathleen Hanna from Bikini Kill. That's what I wanted to sound like. I just didn't have that sort of voice, and so I hated the voice and the image I had for so long. I hated how my voice was so conventional. I was a choir kid, a choir nerd, and my voice worked when it was put in the service of praising Jesus, but put into the service of punk rock it sounded all wrong to my ears.

It's really funny now. When Gossip first started getting reviews, a common sentiment among critics was: *A punk singer who can actually sing!* But back when I was just starting to learn what I sounded like, I hated it. I was a fat kid, a fat girl all my life, and I was always really loud. If a whole room of people were talking, guaranteed I'd be the one who got in trouble. I often tried to make myself smaller, for survival's sake. If my body was going to be big, maybe my voice could balance it out and be softer, sweeter, more gracious. I could be comfortable in my body, but the stress of the world bearing down on me made me not love the loud, wild swell of my voice. It made me mad, not being able to achieve the breathy little-girl sound I heard other girls achieving. On the Little Miss Muffet tape Nathan was selling I sounded tortured, audibly trying to strangle the big, powerful voice I'd been gifted with, trying to stomp it down to something meek and fluffy.

I'd started singing when I was six years old, and I thought I would be a singer when I grew up. It wasn't till I was older that I thought, Oh, I'm too fat to be a singer for a living. No one who looks like me is a singer. I didn't want to set myself up for disappointment. I'll be a nurse like my mom, I thought. When I realized I wasn't going to grow out of my chubby stage, I also realized that I was okay with my body, but I was just about the only one. I wasn't allowed to wear a bikini as a little kid. People called me Bubble Butt because I always had a shelfy little butt, and my bubble butt was not allowed in a bikini. I was always comfortable being a weird kid, a daydreamer, and being fat just seemed to tie in with everything else. It was other people's shame that I found jarring. As I got older, my friends would say things like, *Your face is so pretty, if you just lost weight you'd be so pretty.* My mother was always dieting, and it felt like she was just as ashamed of me as she was of herself. Mom always thought she was ugly, and I always thought it was weird that we looked just like her, all us kids, and she would talk about how ugly she was. How could she do that and not expect her kids to do the same thing? Now I understand she has body dysmorphic disorder—a screwed-up idea of what she looks like—but when I was small it just made me feel bad.

When I got older I was able to say, *Mom, I don't want to hear about it.* And she stopped, but she continued to make comments about herself and other people. After I was about twelve I never heard another thing about losing weight, or about my size. Instead, she said good things about my imagination. She embraced that I could sing and that helped me a lot. I started trying to imagine how I could make singing my job, my whole life. I thought maybe I could make a living as a choir teacher. Not as glamorous as being a singer in a band, but I'd still get to be singing all the time. I couldn't let go of my voice, because it was what I was good at. Hair, and singing. They were the only things I got praise for. I always knew deep in my heart singing was what I would do, even when everything around me was saying it wasn't possible for a fat girl, even when I hated my voice for being too big and too powerful.

From that day with Jeri in front of the talk show forward, I started to change the way I thought about myself. When my mother made comments about fat people, and about her own body, I simply asked her to stop speaking negatively about herself and others, and she never made those types of jokes again. My boyfriend, Anthony, was fat too, so he was supportive, and I decided, after having my confused and ashamed attitude toward my body constantly reinforced, that I would only surround myself with fat-positive people from there out.

One night at Jennifer's house we were on the phone together with Jeri. It wasn't long-distance to talk, and I was excited to be able to just jabber without anyone worrying about catching hell from a parent for a jacked-up phone bill. Jennifer got bored and went into the living room to watch TV, and I stayed in the kitchen. I could hear the canned television laughter in the other room, drowning me out, so I just asked him. *Jeri, are you gay?*

Yes, he said.

I remember the word "fag" coming up in the conversation, and Jeri saying, *It's okay, you can call me that.* I thought about calling Jeri a fag, when so many guys at school hurled the word around. Would it be different if I called him that, "fag"? But he was a fag, if "fag" meant being a boy like Jeri, swishy and queeny and funny and sensitive and in love with boys. Those were all good things, so "fag" was a good word. Jeri had read about boys calling themselves fags in zines like it was a good thing—confounding the bashers— and dykes were doing the same thing. It was some sort of fantastic language revolution. He was refusing to believe that being a fag was a bad thing, just like I was refusing to believe that being fat was shameful.

Okay, fag, I said, careful not to be too loud. I was so happy! Happy and scared for him, and scared for me, but also I felt way closer to Jeri, and I thought, Yup, Jeri came to me and I came to him so we could have each other and deal with this gay bullshit. He had only ever told Kathy about being gay. Quiet Kathy was an excellent secret keeper.

Jeri eventually told Jennifer, and it must have been a relief to finally understand why her boyfriend hadn't ever kissed her. Jeri and Jennifer broke up, and Jennifer became more scarce as we all moved on with our intensifying friendship.

Then, one night, Jennifer tried to kiss Anthony while I was in a deep conversation with Jeri. That was the absolute end of my friendship with Jennifer. As confusing as everything was—and it was confusing—one thing was obvious: you don't go trying to kiss your best friend's boyfriend, even if your best friend is a frustrated dyke.

Jennifer was around just long enough to bring us all together, and then, once we clicked, Jennifer was gone.

After telling me and Jennifer that he was gay, Jeri sort of loosened up and told more people. He told Nathan, who didn't care, and Kathy didn't care, and I sure as hell didn't care. But the stress of coming out was powerful, and the fear Jeri felt was real. Some stupid punk kid found out and told Jeri that he was going to hell. Now, you just can't grow up in apocalyptic Arkansas without half thinking you might actually be going to hell all the time. This might sound nuts to people who weren't raised with such intense, frightening religion, but if that's the air you breathe, it sticks a bit to your insides. Hearing his biggest fear spoken aloud by some asshole was enough for Jeri, in his fragile, spooked coming-out state, to lose it. Jeri collected every gayish thing he owned, a bunch of clothes and magazines, some records, a book, jewelry, anything that struck him as homo—and lots of his stuff did seem gay, because it was all his stuff, and he was gay. He made a big pile of all his excellent weirdo clothes, his pinned-together outfits and homemade accessories, the zines written by boys like him, scared in small towns knowing they're queer—and he set the whole thing on fire in his backyard. Jeri had messed around with a boy, and he was still hung up on him, really liked him, and the single photo that he had of him went into the burning pile too. Afterward he hopped into his car and drove, crying, out to see me. He came to see me a lot back then. The gayness brought me and Jeri together.

That night Jeri and I talked about God, and if God existed, and wasn't God probably just some wild creative energy, something beyond our grasp, something that had made every single thing we knew, including us, and had made us gay, had made Jeri feel pulled toward the boy he'd had his fling with, had made the crazy, wonderful feelings when they kissed. Wasn't that God? The world is too special to have been made by a hateful god. We thought we were so deep that night.

Jeri's mother is a typical Southern mom with the typical Southern name—Sue Ann—and the first real hint that her son might be gay came from a prank Nathan pulled on Jeri's waterbed. Nathan and Jeri had named Jeri's waterbed Vicky, and they liked to pretend it was alive, like some big hungry beast. They would offer Vicky sacrifices. Vicky was a graveyard where pizza crusts went to die. Jeri and Nathan would lodge the crusts between the wooden frame and the mattress. That was exactly the sort of absurd nonsense that made me fall in love with them. Naming a waterbed Vicky and feeding it pizza? It was hilarious. They would also pull off the top sheet, exposing the rubber mattress, and tattoo Vicky in Sharpie. One night, Nathan wrote, MOM, I'M GAY. LOVE, JERI in big black letters.

Sue Ann was making Jeri's bed like a good Southern mom and she saw the message. That was the first time she thought her son might be gay. You might say that Jeri didn't come out to his mom; his waterbed Vicky did it for him.

14

Even though I was spending all my time with Jeri, Nathan, and Kathy, I felt like I was on the outside of their intense friendship. I knew they liked me, so I was way more comfortable around them, but I was still the newcomer. What we needed was a bonding experience to bring me into the fold, and thanks to Nathan, we got one. The night we became a little punk rock family of avant-garde misfits was the night that Nathan told an enormous lie.

Nathan was a notorious liar. There was a sort of famous punk couple who lived in Little Rock, Vic and Stacy. They were so hot and cool and punk that their legend had spread all the way to Judsonia. They were like the Kennedys of Arkansas punk, like royalty. Nathan said he had arranged for us to stay with them, to sleep overnight in their punk rock castle in Arkansas.

Vic and Stacy! Maybe Stacy would take to me in a sweet, big-sister way. She would be so impressed with how I did my hair, she would ask me to style hers, and I would! I would somehow help the impossibly cool Stacy become even cooler, and maybe she would take me in.

Not only was I finally going to catch a glimpse of Vic and Stacy—whom I'd never seen—I was going to sleep at their house! Crash on their floor! It was so thrilling.

I had told my mother that I was going off to Little Rock to stay at the home of an adult couple. She was suspicious.

Punks take care of each other! I tried to explain. We were all in the same big misfit community.

Well, I want you to call me when you get there, and I want to talk to this Vic and Stacy, my mother demanded. It was annoying and embarrassing. Why was she all of a sudden feeling the pull of maternal duty? And why did she have to have a phone?

Fine, I said, *I'll call you. You can talk to them.* The thought of my mother talking to the famous Vic and Stacy was kind of hilarious. She had no idea what legends she'd be speaking to.

The drive to Little Rock in Kathy's car was life changing. It was the first time I was alone with all three of them—Jeri, Kathy, and Nathan. Jennifer was gone for good now. It was just us, cruising along, listening to music and cracking up. I laughed so hard on that drive I peed my polyester pants. Imitations, weird voices, utter nonsense. It was the perfect road trip.

At the Waffle House on the side of the freeway in Little Rock, I sipped at my sweet tea and ate hash browns as we waited for Nathan to come back from the pay phones out front. He was putting in a call to Vic and Stacy, our chaperones. He swung through the glass door and walked back inside the Waffle House, his dirty suit and clanking dog chain raising the eyebrows of the waitresses behind the lunch counter.

What's up?

Nathan shrugged; he was avoiding eye contact behind his heavy, Buddy Holly eyeglasses. *I don't know,* he mumbled. *They're not answering their phone.*

For someone who lied so often you'd think Nathan would be better at it. He'd been so evasive when I'd asked him about Vic and Stacy: what they were like, where they lived, where we would sleep, how he'd met them, if they were excited to meet us. He'd give me a shrug and look at the ground, making me feel like an overeager kid for wanting so much information. Beneath the garish lights of the Waffle House, country music wheezing from the jukebox by the door, it all became clear: Nathan didn't know Vic and Stacy any more than we did. We'd all come down to Little Rock on a lie and had no place to spend the night.

Suddenly the night went from awesome to totally awesome. I could have been mad at Nathan, but I was so high on us being together and feeling like I'd finally lodged myself into their gang. And we'd gotten ourselves to Little Rock! I didn't care if we spent the night at a famous punk's house or at a twenty-four-hour chain diner so long as we were all together.

We left some money on the table and moved on to Vino's, a club where a band was playing. The Delta 72 had a record on Kill Rock Stars, Bikini Kill's label in Olympia, Washington. After the show, we went back to the Waffle House again looking for rancid coffee and sweet tea to keep everyone awake for the drive back. When we pulled into the parking lot a gang of violent jocks started messing with us. We were used to being mercilessly made fun of in public, because it was impossible for us to blend in.

The jocks in the parking lot surrounded us as we sat in Kathy's dumpy little ride. They called us *Fat Farm*. They smacked at the roof of the car with their hands. *Get out of the car, we will kick your ass!* they invited us.

Jeri just sat there, staring out the window. He sat in the front—he always got shotgun because of his height—beside Kathy, and the jocks' faces smeared themselves across the windshield. They smacked their palms on the passenger window, like they were hitting Jeri in the head. If Jeri had gotten out of the car and shown the jocks what they were dealing with, the thugs would have freaked out, but Jeri was a pacifist and a lady. We just huddled inside Kathy's car until they got bored with us and took off. We sat in the silence, everything more quiet without fists pounding on the roof.

We just sat there in the parking lot, listening to music, trying to collect ourselves and get a plan together for the trip home.

The pay phone in the parking lot reminded me I was supposed to call my mother. *Goddamn it!* I didn't want her to worry, but I didn't know what to tell her, and I didn't want to be a freak-bashing target if those jocks were still around. Kathy rolled the car up close to the booth and I made a collect call to Mom and Tom's.

Let me say hello to Vic and Stacy, she said. I hemmed and hawed. Finally, I blurted out, *There is no Vic and Stacy, Mom. Nathan lied.* It didn't occur to me to lie myself, since Mom never cared what I was doing or not doing.

So, you're not anywhere, then? she asked.

No, I'm in the Waffle House parking lot almost getting beat up by jocks. We're going to drink a bunch of coffee and drive home, and I'll sleep in Jeri's waterbed, Vicky.

I'm coming to pick you up, she said. It was so weird when Mom took motherly interest in my well-being. We barely even saw each other—recently she'd resorted to communicating with me via a textbook I'd left at her house. She'd slipped a note into the pages of my science book: *I love you. I know you don't think I do, but I do.* It made me sad.

Mom came all the way to Little Rock to drive me to my sister's house. *I wanted to sleep in Vicky,* I said to Jeri, as I hugged him goodbye, wrapping my arms around him. I wanted to end the night with a slumber party, talking in the dark about deep things, about love and God and our families, about music and clothes and life outside of Arkansas, and about how good it was that Nathan was such a liar because if he hadn't told such a whopper we probably never would have done the road trip to Little Rock, and it had been so much fun. Instead, I'd be fighting off the dark at my sister's place. But I knew that something had shifted that night between me and my friends. We'd become closer on our adventure, and as I pulled away from them in my mother's car, I could feel that I really belonged with them, and they really belonged with me.

I wouldn't have the life I have today, think the thoughts I think, or be myself without them. I'd be pregnant in Arkansas, wondering how come all my babies didn't take my queerness away. Jeri is still my soul mate, and Nathan is still the person who keeps upstaging me with his knowledge of music and culture. I think that, creatively, I keep him grounded, while he keeps my head in the air. Since Kathy was my first full-on girl-crush, that has lodged her in my heart forever. I do think my mom put a spell on me and brought these people into my life, because it feels predestined that I met them when I did.

15

As amazing as life got with my chosen family around me, it took a serious turn for the worse during my senior year of high school. Kathy, Nathan, and Jeri, all three of them older than me, were freed from school, and one by one they did the inevitable—they left Arkansas.

Kathy left first, to go to college. She was always motivated by school and learning, and she wanted to go to Evergreen, in Olympia, Washington. Olympia was home to Kill Rock Stars and Riot Grrrl and everything we worshipped. Evergreen was a state school, not a bourgie, fancy private university, but it was a financial struggle for Kathy to be there. Evergreen was radical and taught its students about politics and encouraged them to be activists and to use art to create social change. At Evergreen you learned about the political dimensions of everything. Your food was political. Your family's economic state was political. Automobiles and gasoline were political. Trash was political. Evergreen was a revelation.

Kathy moved to Olympia by herself, during the longest rainy season they'd ever had. The year Kathy left sunny Arkansas, the

Pacific Northwest skies dumped rain for a record-breaking ninety consecutive days.

Kathy had always been the backbone of our group. She always had a job. Because she was a practical, methodical Virgo, and because of the way she grew up, she needed to work. It preserved her sanity. Nathan, Jeri, and I, we were like, Money, who cares? We'd scrounge or go without. But that attitude made Kathy anxious. She didn't like not knowing where her rent money was coming from, so she took control of her finances.

Kathy and I had grown close in Arkansas. I missed her humor and the special bond we shared with Jeri. Then, about six months into missing her, Nathan and Jeri left. They moved into Kathy's teensy Evergreen dorm room. With no cash, the three of them would make a cheap pack of ramen last for days, rationing it out noodle for noodle.

In phone calls and letters, Jeri and Nathan referred to Kathy's overcrowded dorm room as "the Nest." Apparently, the two boys were sleeping on the floor, in a pile of dirty clothes, like birds that had scraped together a bed from the detritus of the world around them. Jeri found a job doing telemarketing and brought home a paycheck, and Nathan—I don't know how Nathan got by. He must have been getting some help from back home.

Kathy had bought Jeri his plane ticket to Seattle. Kathy always had food, even if it was just a packet of ramen; Kathy always had the rent, even if the house was nothing but a single room stuffed with dirty clothes for sleeping on.

I was a mess without my friends. Everything I'd been staving off, all that I had survived, whatever I hadn't been paying attention to swelled together like a wave to topple and drown me. Without my friends, I felt stuffed back into the lonely part of life, a part I'd thought was gone, but here it was again. I was way too broken to work; I couldn't get it together. I was a senior, and school was ending soon. I would need to get my shit in order. But the more I thought about life, the more overwhelmed I felt. I was haunted by my time at Aunt Jannie's. With my friends gone, and so much time by myself, I felt trapped in my own head, I felt the echoes of everything I'd stuffed away. Without my friends I was shunted back to the old Arkansas, the scary, stifling, trapping place. I had a nervous breakdown.

It started at school. What would have been a sleepy morning for any teenager was—that particular morning—unusually hazy. My eyes couldn't adjust. Light seemed brighter and my body felt like a ton of bricks. During the ride to school my head was a balloon and I still can't remember making my way to class that day. I was sitting at my desk directly behind my best friend at school when the first bell rang and the teacher began to speak, but I couldn't react. It was almost as if I were in a walking coma. My brain was aware and sending messages, but my limbs and mouth couldn't receive them. I tried to reach out and get my friend's attention, but I was paralyzed. Finally my hand made a heavy swipe and came into contact with her. Then my tunnel of vision got smaller and smaller until everything was black. The next thing I knew I was on a gurney gasping for air because I was crying so hard. Of course, because I liked music, had black hair, and was pro-choice everyone assumed I was on drugs. That assumption only fueled my anxiety. I went from school that day to the hospital, where I stayed for five days. My condition worsened and the doctors started running scans on my brain. I lost my ability to speak clearly and developed a stutter that stuck around for three months. The tests all came back negative. The doctors didn't know what to do with me, so I was eventually prescribed antidepressants and sent home.

Some of the physical symptoms lifted over time, though the panic, the clawing fear, remained. I could speak again. Against all odds, I came to and graduated.

It was Kathy, everyone's savior, who got me my one-way ticket to Washington State. I didn't belong in Arkansas, none of us did, and Kathy was a worker, a doer. She'd gotten work at the A&W. Kathy said she could get me a job there too, and if I didn't like

Olympia, if I hated it and wanted to come home to Arkansas, I could just pocket my money and buy a return ticket, which sounded like a foolproof plan. I won either way. It was a deal, so Kathy maxed out her credit card and my three best friends started the search for some hole-in-the-wall we could all afford.

It would be good to get some space between myself and Arkansas. I felt relief just imagining it. My friends' exodus had left a hole in my heart, and I needed to fill it.

I wasn't planning on staying in Olympia for long. I was just coming for a visit, just going to sell some hot dogs, turn around, and come right back to Arkansas, have that baby once and for all, and stay put in what I knew. I didn't break up with Anthony because it wasn't like I was leaving. I was just going on a little vacation to see the friends I missed so much. It was my mother, witchy and psychic, who felt my future the strongest. *You're never coming back,* she said to me flatly. The tone of her voice wasn't good and it wasn't bad. It was just flat, totally neutral. It was the facts. My mother knew how this was going to play out. *Be prepared, because you're not coming home.* I couldn't argue. Something in me was rising up, pulling me to another part of the country. It felt powerful and it ran through my system like a Red Bull. I was going out into my life.

16

High school graduation is a huge racket—both for the company selling caps and gowns and for young entrepreneurs like me. You have to buy invitations to your own goddamn graduation. Then, the idea is that you send graduation envelopes to all your long-lost relatives, and everyone sends you a little money.

When you're like me and half the region is a relation, those dollars pile up. Suddenly I had money to take with me to Olympia. Me, who had never had anything at all. I had a pile of cash and a one-way ticket to the birthplace of Riot Grrrl, where a house full of my favorite people sat, waiting for me to join them.

The night before I left, my mother drove me to my sister's house, and my sister and brother drove me to the airport in the morning. My mother couldn't stand goodbyes, so she stayed behind. I took everything I owned on the plane with me. I told myself that it wasn't because I wasn't coming back. I had just never been on a trip before; I needed all my best stuff for Olympia! Not to mention, my drifter mentality was telling me to keep all of my important things with me. The streets would be full of Riot Grrrls, I would make more friends, I would be with Jeri again, and Kathy, and Nathan!

I know my witchy mom cast a spell on me to get me the fuck out of Arkansas just like I know she cast a spell on me so that I wouldn't get pregnant, try as I might with Anthony. I really believe it was my mom—trying her best to raise us right, to get us all the things she never got, those things that kids keep you from—who made all of it happen. On the way to my sister's house, I sat in her spell that night, inside her oddly silent car.

I'd never been on a plane before that trip. Back then, people could accompany you to the gate, and my brother, sister, and Anthony took me all the way there. My brother had a card for me from my old friend Crystal. They were boyfriend-girlfriend then, and they're still together today. The card read: *I can't believe you're going to Seattle!* There was a calling card tucked inside for me to make long-distance calls back to Arkansas. *I am,* I thought. *I am really, really going.*

My siblings and I have such a special love between us. We don't tell one another that we love one another very often at all, but we always feel it. Our love is there, and it's strong, and I could feel it when they sent me off. I knew that they had done everything they could to make sure I had all the things I wanted, including a shot at life outside Arkansas. I've always been different from my brothers and sisters. They figured out how to build good lives on the site of a lot of pain. They were happy to see me go not because they wouldn't miss me, but because they always knew I would go. It was rare to leave Judsonia, and I was rare, and everything made sense. They wanted me to have the biggest life I could have.

My sister Akasha especially made sure I had everything I needed. She had had to learn about college all by herself. She got herself up every morning as a teenager and made sure we both got our asses to school. She got absolutely straight A's. She was a math and science genius like my two big brothers. She filled out her own financial aid forms to get herself to college. She wanted us to go to Ole Miss together. She intended for us to do that. Instead she went to community college in Beebe, Arkansas, and put me on a plane to Washington State, out into the world.

17

I showed up in Olympia at the very end of the 1990s, thinking
that there were only fifteen punk kids in any town. I was so naïve;
I thought Kill Rock Stars was a tape distro, like what Nathan
was doing but cooler. I'd never actually read *Sassy*. I only got the
trickle-down from other kids who could afford the magazine, so
I didn't realize how enormously the scene had blown up. I didn't
realize how conceptually unprepared I was to be in Olympia until
I landed there. I really thought every punk scene was the same,
and that the only difference with Olympia was there'd always be
something to do. And that was true—compared to Searcy there
was always something to do. It doesn't mean it was always fun or
good, but we always went, Kathy, Jeri, Nathan, and I.

The house Kathy had scored for us was disgusting. It was disgusting before we moved in, because these carny punks who blew
fire had lived there and had really let the house go to shit, the way
only a true punk house can go to shit. Perhaps you've never heard
of a carny punk before. Let me explain. It's very much like what
would happen if a crusty punk married a Ringling brother. Luck-

ily, I'd lived with Aunt Jannie and was used to a gnarly mess. It wasn't a big deal. I shared a foldout couch with Jeri, in the living room, already accustomed to not having my own bedroom. Six of us lived in the place—me, Kathy, Jeri, Nathan, the drummer from Little Miss Muffet—Joey Casio—and a boy named Erin. It was only a two-bedroom house, but every bit of space was commandeered as someone's bedroom.

We were all still underage—Kathy, the oldest, was just twenty—so we would go to the big supermarket in town, Ralph's Thriftway, and shoplift bottles of wine. Stealing food is one thing, but the risk of getting busted grows significantly when you're stealing heavy, cumbersome bottles of booze. The most savvy of us could walk into a Goodwill without a bag and walk out with two stolen bags completely full of pilfered goods. I'd only shoplift little things—a little food, some eyeliner, some lip gloss. But I knew people who could shoplift three or four bottles of wine at once, shoving them in a coat or dropping them in a bag. Nathan, on the other hand, was notoriously bad at it. He would get busted trying to nick a piece of gum.

The whole carny punk house was living off the food Kathy and I could take from the A&W. As promised, Kathy had gotten me a job there, and it kept us all fed for a while. We dined almost exclusively on corn dog nuggets and chicken strips dunked in radioactive yellow honey mustard sauce. Everyone was eating the skanky meat products except Joey Casio, who was vegan and hoarded green beans. It was like a backwoods Southern experience of college dorm living.

In order to get downtown, where the shows were, we had to make it down an enormous hill. We'd wear roller skates and just zoom down it, right into the heart of Olympia. Of course we fell on our asses all of the time, speeding down the steepest hill in town. Jeri and I were the least adept. We'd be drunk on wine, in our roller skates, on our way to some show we'd heard about. At the time, in Olympia, there was this one wine called Night Train that everyone was drinking. Night Train makes Mad Dog look like Cristal. That said, it was especially easy to steal. Imagine grape bubblegum and battery acid. Now mix that with bile and you understand the flavor of my first year in Olympia. It was so gross, but it was fun too.

You couldn't even buy alcohol where I was from—my county, White County, was dry. You had to drive an hour and a half to buy a bottle of anything. In Olympia alcohol was sold casually, and every kid was carrying a Coke bottle filled with whiskey, vodka, or rum, or all three mixed together.

The culture shock continued; Olympia had bagels! We didn't have bagels in Arkansas. You could order vegetarian food all over town! It was so crazy to me—a place with so many vegetarians, the restaurants made special dishes for them? Being in Olympia was like going off to college. It's where I got my education. For eample, before I got to Olympia, I didn't get the concept of touring bands, how they need money badly because they're living on the road and gassing their vans. I thought it was just one big party. I didn't get it, and no one made me feel that more acutely than Nathan.

I respected Nathan, and thought he was hilarious, but Nathan was also a royal pain in the ass. He was like the worst big brother and little brother combined. Too cool plus a compulsive liar. He'd accepted me into the group, but not with the warmth and depth of Kathy and Jeri. He continued to hold me at bay, like I just hadn't totally proved myself yet, and probably never could.

Olympia was a town crawling with music. I was new to the whole punk scene, and my only previous window into music culture were the magazines—like *Rolling Stone*—that I only got my hands on once in a long while. My knowledge of Olympia's music scene was limited, to say the least. Imagine how surprised I was to see Rachel Carns just walking down the street. At that time it was only

about five years after Kurt Cobain's death. People weren't fetishiz-
ing his suicide yet. I was at a party, and Tobi Vail from Bikini Kill
was there. We were joking around, Jeri and Nathan and I—*This
shit is grunge,* we were goofing. *Kurt Cobain is going to show up, this
party is so grunge!* Tobi Vail overheard us laughing and got really
upset. We couldn't possibly be at a party with people who had
known Kurt Cobain? But we were. With people who had known
him, dated him, played music with him.

You know, he was a real person, Tobi Vail said. We shut up, embarrassed. At the time I'd had no idea they'd known each other,
let alone been close. Truly, I was in culture shock. It was so crazy.
It blew my mind right open. These true icons of the '90s weren't
just real people, they were my new neighbors.

Olympia was all-encompassing. I was still dating Anthony, even
though I had basically forgotten about him, and people would
often ask me if he was coming out to stay with me. I couldn't
imagine that happening.

Not only was Arkansas fast receding, Olympia seemed to fold
time. Everything was so distracting, there was always so much to
do, before I knew it days had passed, then weeks. It wasn't that
I made a decision to stay in Olympia as much as I just never got
around to going back to Arkansas. Something was happening to
me. I was starting to live my life, I guess.

I knew Anthony had a girlfriend on the side, and it didn't bother
me. Anthony was like a backup plan. If something bad happened,
if Olympia suddenly didn't work out, I could go back and have babies. Only Anthony had moved on too. Technically he was cheat-
ing on me, and I didn't even care because I was so happy to be
away from Arkansas, doing something different.

When I called Anthony and he said he wanted to break up, I
knew not to fight it. Something inside me rose to accept my life,
and I just said okay. What was severed was bigger than our high

school romance. Now there was nothing left in Arkansas for me to go back to. I walked out onto the porch, where Kathy and Nathan were hanging out with Joey Casio, and I told them what happened. *You should stay,* they all agreed.

Jeri and Nathan had brought their band, Boy Pussy USA, from Arkansas to Olympia. With Boy Pussy USA there was always an elaborate plan. One day I came home and found all my blush completely used up. Jeri and Nathan had thought up a new sort of performance. They had used my makeup to create fake sunburns all over their bodies and pretended to be a Christian homo couple just back from a tropical vacation. They wore short shorts, tank tops, and were covered head to toe in my cheap red blush. They were booked that night at a pool hall that was also a laundromat where we did our laundry sometimes. Jocks hung out at the billiard hall—imagine that—so when Boy Pussy USA got booked for a show there, they devised their sunburned-homo plan to antagonize the jocks.

Olympia was full of misfits from other places who had never had the luxury of a gang to back them up. It felt powerful to storm into a full bar and have just as many punks there as jocks. Perhaps we were cocky troublemakers. But, to us, we were empowered in a situation that had been beyond our control for so long.

And so sexism, racism, and homophobia were dealt with on a whole new, confrontational plane in Olympia. I grew up with bigotry all around me in Arkansas, but the tensions in Olympia, between the regular logging-town folks who came into the city to go to the nightclubs and the freaky punk queers who lived in Olympia, exerted a giant influence over the city. There was a lot of anger and persecution, much of it taking the form of fag-bashing. As usual, Nathan got harassed more than anyone I knew, even though he wasn't gay. One time he got jumped by three boys who pulled him by his scarf onto the ground and started kicking him, calling him a faggot. They kicked him in the head, just a block from where we were living.

That night when Boy Pussy USA got to the pool hall/laundromat, things didn't escalate. It was just funny to watch a bunch of jocks standing around totally confused. No one really knew what to make of Nathan and Jeri. What else was new?

One afternoon at the beat-up carny punk house on Percival Street, Boy Pussy USA were practicing down in the basement. One of the reasons there was such a music explosion in Olympia was how cheap it was to rent a house with a basement that you could convert into a practice space or recording studio. Everyone's basement had instruments stuffed into its dusty corners. On this one day Kathy, who had never played drums in her life, joined Nathan in the basement and started messing with Jeri's drums. She hollered, *Beth, you should come sing in our blues band!* It was a boring day. We had time to kill, and, on a whim, that was how we killed it.

We put together three songs—"Heartbeats," "Say My Name," and "Tough Love." Then Nathan set up a show. We only had three weeks to prepare for it, which freaked out Kathy but didn't bother me. I just didn't take myself seriously enough to care. Plus none of the other bands we were playing with were serious, either. The show was at a space called 510 Columbia. (It's an antiques store now; Olympia has turned into a town of Thai restaurants and antiques stores.) Our debut was opening for Boy Pussy USA's Halloween incarnation, Zombie Beat. It was an honor.

There were only a few people at the show that night, but that was no surprise. We didn't really ever expect anyone to be there because there were so many things going on in Olympia, people were pretty spoiled for choice. We had fun with or without an audience. Kathy, who could not bear to have anyone look at her while she played, had asked Joey Casio to stand onstage in front of her drums so no one could see her. She was too nervous. The most nerve-racking thing for me was that Rachel Carns was in the audience. She was so easy to spot in the thin crowd, with her dark hair and dramatic, Sharpied eyebrows, listening and watching intensely. That made my day. I didn't care if anyone else was there. Rachel Carns! Watching me sing! When we had finished our three songs she helped me climb off the stage, taking my hand and planting a kiss on it. I truly didn't care about what might happen to me for the rest of my life. Pretty much nothing was going to top Rachel Carns kissing my hand as she helped me off the stage. It remains one of the most amazing moments of my life.

After our set, Zombie Beat—Jeri and Nathan's latest hilarious persona—played. Jeri would pretend he was a zombie, and Nathan begged the audience not to clap, because it made the zombie so mad. Of course everyone would keep clapping, to enrage the zombie. The act required fake blood, and the best stuff we could get our hands on was the free taco sauce packets at Taco Bell, so that's what we used. When I jumped onstage to be attacked by zombie Jeri, the sauce went into my eyes and I felt like I had been pepper-sprayed, it hurt so bad. Thank god Gossip had played first because I don't know how I would have been able to sing after being Taco Bell pepper-sprayed.

Five months after opening for Zombie Beat, the Gossip set list had swelled from three to five songs, and we were playing around Olympia all the time. I had grown more confident, letting myself begin to really love the performance of singing, taking all that energy from the crowd and hurling it right back at them.

In 1999 K Records asked us to do an EP. Calvin Johnson started K in the early '80s. Calvin was Olympia's premier indie rock overlord. K's motto was "Exploding the teenage underground into passionate revolt against the corporate ogre since 1982." He'd started K just to get his friends' music out into the world and wound up with one of the biggest, most respected anticorporate DIY indie punk labels ever. And Gossip was in the right place at the right time. We said yes immediately. The EP featured "Jailbreak," one of the first songs we ever wrote, plus three other songs. We were labelmates with the wild electro-art feminists Chicks on Speed, with the cult classic avant-garde musicians Mecca Normal, and with Calvin's own band, Beat Happening.

Shortly after we recorded the EP, Sleater-Kinney asked us to go on tour with them. Carrie Brownstein had seen us play at some house party and thought we would fit well into their tour lineup. She passed the invitation to Nathan, the most social member of our band.

People were astounded that Sleater-Kinney had invited us to tour with them, but I didn't get why everyone was so worked up. Sleater-Kinney was a punk band to me. I had listened to *Call the Doctor* on repeat, and I knew it was an honor to go on tour with a band I loved so much, but I just hadn't realized how big the indie punk world was.

Our first show in Minneapolis was at 7th Street Entry, where part of *Purple Rain* had been filmed. The max capacity was nearly the population of my entire hometown. We were suddenly playing real venues, with tech people who treated us like we were real musicians, and out there beyond the stage—a real audience. Hundreds of people.

On that six-week tour every venue we played was legit, not a laundromat or a friend's living room. We didn't have to worry about people showing up, because Sleater-Kinney drew tons of fans to every show. They took such good care of us—in New York they paid us a bonus. To see the country that way—to tour as a band like that for the first time—was insane. Our first show ever in San Francisco was at the Fillmore. It sounded so intimidating, but the less intimate the setting, the easier it was to play a show. The energy is more spread out in a place like that, less concentrated. For me, the intimacy of our early shows was nice, but it's *really* nice to have a lot of people around you. You can get away with a lot more.

We drove alongside Sleater-Kinney in a Mazda MPV—a small minivan. Our driver was a seventeen-year-old named Kelly Bakko, and the minivan belonged to her dad. After a while we felt bad just having Kelly, aka Little Kelly, aka Sassy Lassie, as our roadie. We wanted her to have a more glamorous role in the tour, so we made her our dancer. She would stand up on the stage and jerk around in this slow, glitchy way. We didn't pay Little Kelly, because we didn't know we were supposed to. We had no merchandise to sell, because we hadn't put out a record yet. Inside the van, there was no place to put your feet down because we had crammed coolers into all the available floor space, along with Kathy's drums and Nathan's amp, an old Peavey that we joked would die any day, and Gossip would die along with it. The Peavey only had one speaker—it was supposed to have two; it was absolutely busted. On that first tour, all our luggage was stuffed in a case on the roof that Sleater-Kinney called the Hamburger, because it looked like the container a fast-food hamburger comes in. They always knew which minivan we were in because they'd spot the Hamburger bobbing in the sea of vehicles on the highway.

With shows every night, I started to realize how naturally performing came to me. It felt totally normal to be up there on a stage in front of hundreds of people. I was quick-witted. Performing wasn't that different from being a fat fifth grader just trying to keep her friends laughing. At one show a girl clambered onstage holding a dog leash and begging me to leash her up and tug her around the stage like a dog, which was embarrassing for both of us. Instead of letting the situation spiral into a shameful experience, I made a cheesy showbiz wisecrack à la Mae West—*Come see me after the show*—and sent the girl and her leash on their way. Disaster averted. The Sleater-Kinney ladies commented on it after the show, impressed by how I'd handled the situation, but it didn't seem like a big deal to me; it was just what came naturally. But slowly things were falling into place. I was getting an understanding of myself in the world. I hadn't known I was a fast thinker. In fact, I thought I was slow. People associate being fat with being slow, and I probably internalized that. It wasn't until I was onstage that I realized I thought fast on my feet. That was how I'd learned to deal with the world. It's why I love that one jackass in the audience who needs to steal a little bit of my spotlight, usually by shouting stupid insults. I love a heckler! They switch on my creativity and I don't even care that I'm being made fun of, because it's like this great game that we're playing—one that I always win.

My size has helped make me an amazing performer too. The cliché of the Funny Fat Friend: I absolutely was that character—I *am* that character. At school, I had to beat people to the punch, making fun of myself before they got the chance to make fun of me. I had to be more charming, more sharp, more hilarious. Fat kids are always trying extra hard to get people to like them, because so many people are ready to hate them on sight. And at the same time, fat kids learn pretty quickly not to give a fuck. It's a complicated bag of tools I acquired, and I've put them all to work onstage—wit, thinking on my feet, not giving a fuck. I have survival skills that other people don't have. I feel sorry for people who hit thirty, thirty-five years old and find themselves with more weight on their bones, for people who've had skinny privilege and then have it taken away from them. I have had a lifetime to adjust to seeing how people treat women who aren't their idea of beautiful and therefore aren't their idea of useful, and I had to find ways to become useful to myself.

I don't know if Nathan or Kathy understood what a big deal it was to be touring with Sleater-Kinney, or that it was the start of the next significant cycle in all our lives. I know I didn't. But it was a big deal. When you're on tour you're not thinking, Oh let's do this again! You're just going show to show doing what people ask you to do, and having fun. It didn't dawn on me that this is what some people did for a living. In my world, people worked fast food, got greasy serving corn dogs, put on a smock and made corporate sandwiches. Maybe if you were lucky you scored a waitress or bartender gig where you could collect tips. But making a real, sustainable living traveling around in a band, playing punk shows every night? Not part of my reality.

Living in Olympia had warped my brain into believing that all bands were made up of queer punk feminists who understood fat politics. It was like all the bands in Olympia were soundtracking a shared revolution; most everyone understood that things were fucked, and, to some degree, you could trust that your musical peers were on the same page as you politically. Outside Olympia, people were homophobic, fatphobic; full of unchecked racism and sexism; thought poor people were trashy. As Gossip kept bringing me deeper into the mainstream music industry, I came into contact with more people, bands, and labels that might share the punk aesthetic, but not the politics that drew me to punk in the first place. I was so naïve, thinking everyone in bands was all the same, all little angry feminist queers who'd just busted out from our oppressive small-town homes. No way.

While being aware and radical was normal in Olympia, being identified with queerness, feminism, and fat-positivity sometimes holds bands back in other places. Being associated with a political agenda can totally pigeonhole a band. But then, there are always people and publications who support radical bands even more, partly because they are so political. To this day, Gossip's appearance on the cover of *Punk Planet* magazine remains one of the things I'm proudest of. *Punk Planet* helped punk keep its money where its mouth was. Its approach to punk was motivated at heart not by fashion or just music, but by an ethic that valued an equitable approach to any kind of cultural production. An interview with Thurston Moore and reviews of random seven-inch records by Midwestern teen punk bands could be sandwiched next to articles on feminism, media criticism, and visual art. RIP, *Punk Planet*.

· · ·

We came back from tour a little different each time, but the home-coming was always the same: the frantic rush of having to find a job and then the halfhearted struggle to keep it. The A&W wouldn't take me back, so after opening for Sleater-Kinney for six weeks I came home and got hired at Subway.

Working at Subway kind of ruled—it was right next to my house, so if I had to be at work at 9:30 I'd roll out of bed at 9:25. I've had a lot of disposable fast-food jobs over the years, and I actually felt lucky to have scored the role as a Subway "sandwich artist"; jobs in Olympia are really hard to come by. The economy there sucks. If you don't land a state job, it's pretty much food service or nothing. After Subway, I worked at Bagel Brothers, then at Metro, this stupid clothing store where you can find a sexy nurse outfit, or a French maid outfit, things like that—really annoying stuff. I worked there a total of five days before getting fired. After Metro I was hired at Batdorf & Bronson, a highly coveted coffee-shop job. Batdorf & Bronson offered stability. It was a grown-up job by Olympia stan-dards, meaning you could get health insurance and a 401(k). I'd been around town long enough by then. In Olympia, that meant you got the good coffee-shop job. The point being: if you think com-ing back from a successful tour is glamorous, you are dead wrong.

Despite Olympia's shitty job situation, it was a really magical place. The cost of living was so low that everyone was able to sort of skate by on random jobs and still have enough free time to steal their roommate's blush and dress up as gay vacationers in nonsensical performance bands. What the town lacked in eco-nomic opportunity, it more than made up for with a community of supportive, innovative people who created a great art and music scene. There were always tons of people starting crazy projects, or willing to be enthusiastic about your crazy project.

· · ·

Soon after we got back from tour, Kill Rock Stars asked if they could put out our full-length record. That's when we started thinking that we could really be a band. Everyone was acting like we had already made it, but it was still so hard to take ourselves seriously.

The Kill Rock Stars office was literally across the street from our house. I used to go over and hang out after work, loitering and getting in the way and eavesdropping on town gossip. One day, when Nathan was doing the same, they just asked him if we wanted to put out a record. Nathan had already promised our first album to K, but I say that's what you get for doing business with Nathan. I had no complaints about the switcheroo—I really think KRS is the best indie label around. Kill Rock Stars! It was super exciting. They'd put out Bikini Kill *and* Kathleen Hanna's spoken-word CD, plus their label had Riot Grrrl bands like Bratmobile, and the British queers Huggy Bear, and they had even worked with Corin Tucker from her rough old band Heavens to Betsy all the way up to Sleater-Kinney. Not to mention Elliott Smith. Not to mention Nirvana. And now Gossip would be part of that legacy.

KRS hooked us up with Paul Schuster, who recorded bands at his house. I recorded my vocals in his bathroom, the rest of the band recorded their parts in his bedroom, and that was that. We had an album: *That's Not What I Heard*. I was nineteen years old.

Once we had an album to promote, we had the incredibly good fortune to get picked up by a booking agent for Sonic Youth and Sleater-Kinney. Things started happening really fast. I didn't realize how unusual it was to have things come our way so easily. They booked us our first headlining tour, in the United States. Our dancing roadie, Little Kelly, drove us across the USA once more in her dad's minivan. U.S. Tour Round II; the hilarity ensued. Our entire band was still too young to drink. We only played under-twenty-one shows back then so that kids who were our age and younger could come see us. Most of the shows on the

Sleater-Kinney tour had been all-ages too, but occasionally there would be a show in a bar and we'd all have to hang around outside the venue until it was time for us to perform. Gossip never played twenty-one-plus shows until we'd all turned twenty-one, and then—how soon we forgot!

Our own tour was a lot smaller than the giant Sleater-Kinney one we'd just come home from, but it was every bit as fun. We were playing to much tinier crowds of about fifty people. Nathan would get paid out after the show and split the hundred-and-fifty-dollar guarantee among the three of us. It never occurred to us to have a band fund or anything. We just let whoever went into the gas station pay for the gas, and it worked out okay. I remember sitting around after a show, collecting my cut of the money, and Nathan saying, *We just made more than what we would have made working an eight-hour day.* It was true. Eight hours at minimum wage came out to about forty-eight dollars.

We felt rich. We *were* rich. It really did feel so luxurious. And we did it all pretty much ourselves. With a cellphone, compliments of KRS, and a binder full of directions, courtesy of our booking agent, we were turned loose on the country. That binder of directions looped us around the USA and guided us safely back to Olympia, our pockets full of road cash and our mouths full of stories for everyone we'd left behind. It was a charmed situation.

For a long time I really shortchanged us. I felt scared to admit that there was something special about our band and I chalked up our growing success to luck. I just couldn't believe that my life could be heading in such an amazing direction, and that my bandmates and I were responsible for making that happen. That type of success just wasn't something that happened to people like me.

Back in Arkansas, my mom's phone had been cut off yet again, so it was hard to stay in touch with her. I could reach her at work, but it had taken me forever just to let her know I'd made it to

Washington safely. While I was on tour, Akasha had started dating this really stable guy who had a phone, so she was the one I was in touch with most often. During that time, we grew closer and closer, and she even named her baby after me. If you'd told me something like that would happen back when we were kids, I'd have laughed at you and called you crazy, but Akasha's love for me was deep, and got stronger as we got older. Akasha sent care packages in the mail: a box of Tuna Helper and three liters of Mountain Dew, a fake Christmas tree box all crisscrossed with duct tape, full of food purchased back in Arkansas. Sometimes she'd clean out her pantry at home and send me everything.

When I was working at a T-shirt shop, starving, Akasha called me on the store phone one afternoon, and I started to tell her how hungry I was. She immediately offered to order me a pizza and have it delivered to my house. I was floored. It seemed magic, like my sister herself was going to materialize on my doorstep with a big steamy pizza in her hands. I was delirious with hunger, but she did it. She used her credit card to get a pizza delivered to my house in Olympia from her phone in Arkansas. That's the kind of stuff she'd do for me. Back then, how I was living, I'd go three days without even realizing I hadn't eaten. Or I'd just eat a packet of ramen every other day. I lost a lot of weight in Olympia, since I didn't have enough money to feed myself. That, coupled with my new active lifestyle—roller skating down massive hills then stumbling back up them again—was like being on a crash diet.

Once Gossip started hitting the road, money got even more scarce. I had to quit my job in order to go on tour, and that quickly became my lifestyle—get a shitty job, make it work, ditch it to go on tour, come back, and scramble for another shitty job. I made some money on the road, but not so much that I wouldn't have to put my whole life back together from scratch when I returned.

Things continued along at breakneck speed. We put out another EP, *Arkansas Heat,* after our tour and followed it up with our next album, *Movement,* which was a really exciting project.

John Goodmanson produced it, and he had produced Bikini Kill's *Singles*, possibly the most genius collection of songs of all time. It was amazing to work with someone of that caliber. *Movement* became our first grown-up record. We went on a bunch of six-week U.S. tours to promote it.

In Olympia everyone was an artist with a day job. You had to pay your rent somehow, and your art wouldn't do it. I never felt like I was living two lives—the successful, touring musician and the sandwich artist—until the release of *Standing in the Way of Control*, when the band blew up in London. The album was an unexpected hit, and the music magazine *NME* named me number one on their 2006 Cool List. That's when things got weird.

In England I hung out with Grace Jones in her hotel room, became friends with Kate Moss, and met the Raincoats. I was asked to do a song with Jarvis Cocker from Pulp. There were honest-to-god paparazzi following me around. Having those experiences in England, and then returning home to the shitty rental house I shared with Jeri and my blind, ferocious cat—*that* felt like living a double life. But earlier, when we were touring the States, playing to crowds of fifty kids, and then returning to our minimum wage jobs in Olympia, that was not a double life. That was normal. I was recognizable; I was in a band good enough to go on tour, we got reviewed in *Spin*, but those things weren't necessarily huge.

At some point I started to understand that, even though we weren't getting big write-ups in magazines, Gossip was what I did for a living. I had to fill in the gaps with shitty jobs less and less. I was sustaining myself. When I called home, my family didn't act like it was too big a deal. My brother was playing music in a traveling band too; we had other family members who'd been musicians. My life wasn't that unusual. It honestly wasn't until *Standing in the Way of Control* that my family started thinking that maybe I'd be doing this forever.

18

Olympia was a great place to be queer. Riot was a subculture that gave girls a lot of room to figure out who they were sexually. Lots of girls were queer, and lots of those queers lived in Olympia. Once I had let go of Anthony I was ready to get real about who I was. But the more I got into it, the more complicated it all seemed to become.

I had a hard time feeling like a lesbian, because I didn't feel like I was attracted to girls. The girls I liked were always more like boys than girls, and I thought all lesbians only liked girls who were just like them. Butches went with butchy girls, and femmes went with femmes. I liked girls who were so different from me they were like a whole other species.

Enter Melanie.

We met at the mall, back when I was working at the A&W hot dog place. She was working at a cinnamon roll place. There was a mall directory that had all the stores' and snack counters' numbers. Melanie looked up A&W and rang me. We started talking all the time, and we'd each be in the back of our shops on the telephone, talking to each other and ignoring customers, and then Melanie would say, *Let's go to the counter and wave to each other,* and we'd put down the phone and run over to our registers and stick our hands up, smiling, goofy and giddy. Eventually we started hanging out after work. I would stay the night at her place and in the morning we'd get up and go to the mall together, squeezing our hands goodbye beneath the glare of the food court lights.

After we'd been going out for a little, Melanie asked me to move in with her and I said I would, as long as I could take Jeri with me. I packed up Jeri and moved him out of the carny punk house and into Melanie's. We all lived together for almost two years. But something about it wasn't right. I felt like I was playacting the life I thought lesbians were supposed to have. I was trying to be what I thought a lesbian should be—committed, domestic, nested, and not too feminine.

The whole time I was with Melanie, I didn't understand I was a femme. For me, and for a lot of women, my personal feminist evolution mirrored pieces of the larger feminist journey through history—specifically the historical waves of feminism. So, it wasn't a surprise that my early interpretation of feminism and my new lesbian identity included a rejection of anything that had been socially deemed "feminine." It was my own personal bra-burning phase. With the (unfortunately still radical) feminist idea that a woman's worth is not determined by how she looks comes a natural suspicion of everything society tells women they *have* to do in order to be pretty, and therefore valuable. Things like shaving, wearing makeup, dressing in skirts, wearing heels, and slipping into lingerie all fell under that category, so I cut my hair short and put on jeans. Looking back, I was trying to be a butch lez, which was the only sort of identifiable lesbian I saw growing up—women with short hair who looked boyish.

The tyranny of beauty was an oppression the feminists had escaped. I didn't want to be a fool. I knew that a lot of people would think I wasn't even in the beauty-contest running because of my size. It seemed best, maybe, to throw that baby right out with all the shitty bathwater. I could just say goodbye to femininity and all its sexy accoutrements.

Soon enough, though, these philosophies weren't enough to keep me inspired. I loved doing my hair, playing dress-up, making up my face. I never did it to win the hearts or attentions of men or women, I did it because it was fun, it captured my imagination, it made me feel great about myself when I was all done up in some new way that no one had thought of doing before. Self-expression, even feminine self-expression, was not my enemy. The real enemy was the ideals that women are expected to live up to, and suddenly that limited style of feminism just felt like another ideal breathing down my neck. I wanted to fight oppression and be powerful, and I wanted to do it in a cute dress and a bouffant hairdo. That's how I felt powerful.

In my little punk, queer, '90s feminist world, no one wanted to feel weak, but women are always portrayed as weak. So a sub-cultural ideal of boyishness ruled at the time. We wanted to look tough, not froofy. Now it all feels like another form of misogyny—*Don't be a "girl"*—but back then it felt like the right way to rebel against the mainstream. And so I went underground. I felt like a little boy who sneaks into his mom's makeup bag and plays dress-up when no one's looking. I would do my hair up all ratted and glam and then brush it out before I left the house because I thought I was supposed to be more butch.

I was a closeted femme! And I wasn't alone. Butches transform into femmes all the time in the queer scene. A waitress I know who started out super butch made a transition over the course of two years, and now she has long hair and wears lipstick every day. It's really great, actually, to watch someone slowly letting herself become who she truly is supposed to be. I wonder if anyone had their eye on me while I slowly unraveled my false butch persona and let the real femme out, letting my hair get bigger and bigger each day, teasing it with a skinny comb, hitting it with furtive blasts of hairspray. Lip gloss led to lipstick led to lipstick topped with lipstick. Mascara led to eyeliner led to eye shadow. I'm not the sort who thinks that heels or hairdos are inherently feminist, but the idea that women can be trusted to choose their own forms of self-expression certainly is.

Even though Melanie wasn't my perfect match, and might have been a little happier with me if I really had been a butch, it was still super exciting to have a girlfriend. It was a Big Deal. I've been kind of a serial monogamist for a long time, which I'm okay with, but it also means I don't have a lot of experience in the dating world. I never got to have my wild time of making out with different people. I just hooked right up with a girl who really wanted to settle down. Melanie was only twenty-one, but she knew what she wanted. She talked about babies a lot. I would be like, *Babies? Whoa.* I just didn't want what she wanted. Every time I left for a tour she'd be upset. She didn't like me going out. I was just nineteen years old, still fresh out of Arkansas, and all I wanted to do was run around and be out in the world, having fun. Melanie was really sweet, she just had her own things she wanted to do and she was serious about them.

It was sad how things ended with Melanie. I cheated on her. I made out with her best friend, Kristin. That broke us up, then we got back together, but it was never the same. Eventually we started dating other people.

I started dating Freddie, and it was the sweetest romance, but it was complicated by my dying relationship with Melanie. I first met Freddie at a Gossip show. He was standing in the front and he was so distracting that I had to perform way on the other side of the stage from him. Freddie is a boy. I'd met butch girls before, tomboyish girls who were naturally masculine, but Freddie was something else. He's transgendered. There are many, many different ways people deal with being transgendered. Some people get full medical transitions and become as physically like the gender they identify with as possible. A lot of people can't afford the procedures it takes to go that route, and others just don't feel that they need to. Freddie felt like he already *was* a boy, he didn't need a bunch of doctors and surgery to make him look like what the world *thought* a boy was supposed to look like. But Freddie's identity, and transgendered identity, for that matter, is not for me to define. All I knew was that Freddie was dreamy, and he gave me shivers.

I was still with Melanie when Freddie asked me out, and the whole gay dating thing was so new and confusing, I couldn't tell what was a platonic hangout and what was romantic. He asked me to hang out with him and I was like, *Okay, we'll hang out.* I didn't know he'd been asking all my friends about me, unsure of whether he should ask me out. My situation with Melanie was confusing to everyone. I'm pretty sure that no one had ever had a crush on me before. I was always the one who asked people out, but Freddie asked me. We went to the Rib Eye, one of two places that stay open late in Olympia. I sat across from him, drinking a Mountain Dew. I was broke as a joke. Freddie was very attractive, very dapper. He wore a leather jacket with a scarf and was already dating two other people at that time. At the Rib Eye he ate a sandwich, and in the car on the way home afterward he said, *Well, you could say this was not unlike a date.* I made a noise that was some cross between a squeal and a goodbye, and I literally jumped out of his car and ran inside my house. That was how things began with Freddie, and how things with Melanie ended.

At that time, my romantic life was stuck in an odd limbo. I was living with Melanie, but we were more like roommates than girlfriends. Both of us understood that I was never going to be the kind of girl she wanted, but we were scared to let go. Meanwhile, Freddie was courting me in a strangely old-fashioned way.

I was working at a T-shirt shop called Teed Off. People made bulk T-shirt orders, like for a Little League sports team. They phoned the order in, and the T-shirts never came through. My main task at Teed Off was covering for my boss, a cracked-out miserable little man who cashed everyone's checks, took the money, and never came up with the T-shirts. I'd hold off the angry customers as long as I could, stalling them, hoping the shirts would show up or that they'd give up, but eventually I'd just have to tell them, *I don't think you'll ever get your shirts. And I think we spent your money.* It was ridiculous how many times a day I'd have to answer the phone and talk to these Little League moms. Most of my time was spent fielding complaint calls from angry women, and the rest of the time was spent dusting the inventory of useless crap we sold—stupid shit like rubber duckies with devil horns, or hula girls for your dashboard. I worked eleven hours a day, five days a week, no overtime.

Freddie and I weren't technically dating, not with me still living with Melanie, but he brought flowers to me every day at Teed Off. I don't think I even knew what romance was, but I began to understand, watching Freddie roll up on his motorcycle outside the shop like James Dean, with a fistful of flowers. I didn't know what to do with them—I couldn't bring them home, so I kept them in the bathroom at work, by the sink, and I would go in and look at them when no one was there. I felt like a girl in some John Hughes movie, like I was the poor kid and he was this really beautiful, handsome jock or something. I would sit there in that shitty bathroom in front of the lovely flowers and dream about him.

One day he brought flowers in while Melanie was there. He burst through the doors with the bouquet bright in his hands, and Melanie and I froze behind the counter. We were all speechless. Freddie felt so bad, a wave of it moved over his face. He put the flowers on the counter and he just quietly left the shop. Melanie was shook up by that. She started coming by to visit more, and my miserable little boss picked up on the drama. One day when Melanie was hanging around he came out from the bathroom with his arms full of Freddie's flowers. *Didn't someone bring these by for you?* he asked with mock innocence, the little shithead. *Do you want to keep them?* It wasn't long after that that Melanie and I decided we should break up. I offered to leave, but with me and Jeri all nested in that house, it felt like ours. Melanie moved out instead.

I waited a little while, and finally when I thought I might be ready I called Freddie out of the blue. *Hi,* I said. *Hi, I think I can go on a date with you if you still want to,* and he did.

He made my gender identity make sense to me, and he made my sexual identity make sense to me. With Freddie, he was a top and I was a bottom and he was a boy and I was femme, and it all just made sense. He was really sweet to me. The way he paid attention to my stories—I had never had anyone who listened to me that way before. Freddie is seven years older than me, and when you're nineteen years old, that's a lot. He had train hopped, traveled across the United States that way. He'd had all these sexcapades, hooking up with girls all over the country. He'd done things I'd never heard of. It felt really scary to date someone like that, but it was exciting. He was dreamy and perfect, and I took advantage of the odd power I'd accrued by putting up with bullshit and bounced checks at Teed Off and started sauntering in hours late for my shift after getting it on all night with my new boyfriend.

I've always related to Freddie's choice to not medically transition, because in some ways, it's similar to my attitude toward being fat. My life would be easier if I were thin, if I did what I was supposed to do to have that sort of body. Some people need to make those changes in order to feel safe, but for me it feels like resisting the norm to keep my body as it is naturally. And the way Freddie is about his gender, that he doesn't take testosterone or have surgery to change the body he's got, that's a resistance too. It's a challenge—why shouldn't he be able to have the body he's got and the identity he wants? Since Freddie is male, doesn't that make his body, as is, a male body?

By not changing himself physically, Freddie dares everyone around him to change their bullshit notions about what is male and what is female, and the world gets bigger for everyone. And I feel like, Why can't I have the body I have and do all the things I want to do in this body? Each of us has made a decision to stick by the body we got and make the world change to accommodate *us*.

19

About a year and a half after moving away, I went back to Arkansas to visit. The Sleater-Kinney tour had ended a few months earlier and I was settled in enough to make a short trip. When I got to my mother's house my entire family was there. They had one of those banners made of foil reading WELCOME HOME hanging in the living room. They had never had someone leave and then come back before. No one left. It was exciting for all of them that one of us had gone out into the world. They wanted to hear my stories and shower me with attention and questions and laughter and hugs.

It was wild to see everyone getting older, having kids, and the kids they already had getting older in my absence. People having children will really make you want to be close to your family. You don't want to miss that. And so far, everyone in my family has done such a good job with their kids, which is remarkable considering what things were like for us. People my age in my family aren't having very many babies of their own, which is sort of radical for where we're from. One of my brothers doesn't have any kids, and the others only have two, while Akasha has one. I think that, for all the mess we've created, there was always something special, something a little magical and different, about my family. I'm not surprised my brothers and sisters have broken the cycles of abuse and despair. I don't know who or what to be grateful to—maybe it's Mom's particular magic. I know that a lot of families suffer abuse never break that cycle, and I'm so proud of my siblings for all the revelations and sacrifices that they made to bring them to where they are today. And I could see, when I returned home on that visit, that they were very proud of me as well.

I hadn't been gone very long but Arkansas had changed. It was changing the way every other part of America was changing, even the crappy and forgotten parts. There's a Starbucks now, but I still get my coffee from McDonald's. For so long McDonald's was the only reliable place to get a cup of coffee back home, and I can't shake the habit. They even sell iced coffee now! My cousins couldn't believe I was drinking coffee cold when I was home. It blew their minds. Nobody drinks their coffee cold. Little things like this were giving all of us culture shock. I didn't think twice about drinking some iced coffee, but as I watched everyone around me react it became charged with something bigger. I'd been away, had seen things, done things, and tried things, and I'd been changed by it. That whole revelation got tripped by a dumbass cup of weak and watery chilled coffee, and it was sort of hilarious, but there you go.

My family is amazingly cool, and that visit back to them just reminded me what a weird island of relative sanity they are in the Bible Belt. Even with everything that had happened, even with the shit that has gone unpunished—unacknowledged—by my family, I know how bad it can get out there and I know how lucky I am, truly, to have these people on my side. They are the most important people in the world to me. My siblings and I were always encouraged to put ourselves in other people's shoes. That is such a simple and powerful thing to teach a kid. It teaches them compassion and gives them such a great lens to view the world through.

It shows them how to be open to life and not all shut down against it. I remember being a really little kid and some afterschool special about gays in high school was on the television. My mother stood in the room, watching me watch it. *Just imagine how it feels to be that kid in school,* Mom told me. It always stuck with me, that she said that.

Once I became serious with Freddie, I wanted him to come to Arkansas with me, to see where I'm from and to be able to match all my stories up with faces and places. I trusted him enough to show him my world, and I trusted my family enough to know they would treat him right, and they did not let me down. My whole family respected that Freddie was male and called him "he," no big deal. I don't know if they understand the finer points of transgender identity, but they know how to give a person the respect he requires, they understand dignity and manners.

What they did not understand or respect—what really scandalized my family—was reading in a local Arkansas paper that I didn't believe in God anymore. There is only one sin that is unforgivable in my family, and that is to denounce God. They were worried for my soul, which isn't a bad thing, actually. It's sweet to have a big group of people who love you so much that they are concerned about your afterlife. I don't care if my family thinks I'm sinning, as long as they don't treat me like shit about it.

20

After *Movement* came out Gossip got to go to Scotland. We went with the singer-songwriter Sarah Dougher and this band called the Lollies. Sarah was part of the band Cadallaca with Corin Tucker from Sleater-Kinney, and on her own she wrote beautiful, strong, and folksy songs for her guitar. She was touring her new CD, *The Bluff.*

The Lollies were a U.K. girl group that had blown up after the *NME* named them the best new band in Britain. They were punk and into '60s garage music and generally fell into being a band in the same jokey way Gossip had, so we got along great. The tour was hilarious. In the USA I was still underage, but not in Europe! I drank and smoked myself into oblivion. That was back when I could just bounce back from a night spent getting hammered, without a shame spiral in the morning or giving a shit about anything. That was before touring became hard work. Those days can't last forever, and I was glad I took advantage of my resiliency on that tour.

It was my first time in Britain. We went to Glasgow to play

Ladyfest Scotland and did some shows in little towns throughout the U.K. We went to a working-class place called Hull, and our show there was my favorite U.K. performance to this very day. There weren't any kids at the show, just local blue-collar workers and older lesbians. By the end of the night we had drunk machinist guys screaming Bikini Kill lyrics with us: *"TAKE BACK, TAKE BACK THE REVOLUTION!"*

What was happening then, and what continues to happen, is the longer I sing, the more records we make, the more I am using my real voice. I never knew what pitch was, or what key was, and so many albums later I'm starting to get an idea. As a little kid I wasn't encouraged much in school. My mother did her best, as usual, but her tutoring skills were spread too thin. Lucky for me, she saw my potential. Overhearing my Munchkinland versions of "Like a Virgin" or "Girls Just Want to Have Fun," Mom would pop into the room, grab hold of my nose, and say, *Not through the nose, from the gut!* snapping her fingers, counting, *One, two, three, four!* Teaching me the bare basics of rhythm, projection, and confidence. I still can't totally tell if something sounds "pitchy," but I keep learning, and when I'm performing and recording I find myself applying the things I've picked up, skills I've learned from other singers I've met along the way, tricks I've learned from people helping us with our albums, and stuff I figured out on my own, almost intuitively, from singing all day every day for so many years. When we recorded *Movement* I didn't know anything about singing; by the time we recorded *Standing in the Way of Control* I understood a lot more.

In 2008 we recorded *Music for Men,* and we had the luxury of taking as much time as we needed to record. It gave me the space to understand how to use my voice even more fully than on our other records, which was amazing. But I could feel, even during those sessions, that I had gotten to the heart of my true voice yet, and I also hadn't figured out how to take all the different ways I'd learned to sing and use them together. I'm able to do a lot of different styles of singing and I don't think that's true for all vocalists. I've become so comfortable with my voice, and I can accept that it's *good*, and I use it to do what comes naturally instead of forcing it into some girl-singer box. I don't restrict myself anymore out of being scared about what I should or shouldn't sound like. And I've been able to teach young singers what it's taken me so many years to figure out at Rock 'n' Roll Camp for Girls. I'm helping to teach them to take the less painful road of accepting their differences and embracing their one-of-a-kind sound from an early age.

I have been lucky enough to volunteer at Rock Camp for one week each summer, teaching vocals, and it's always an incredible experience. The girls at the camp are ages eight to eighteen, and the instructors are mostly self-taught, do-it-yourself female or transgendered folks. We teach them every aspect of making music we can think of. Rock Camp started in Portland, Oregon, back in 2002. Some of those original kids are now young adults, and many of them have come back to the camp as volunteers. It's a radical environment that teaches kids to know and accept and love themselves, to give themselves permission to be exactly who they are. If anyone thinks that music and feminism are not important, that Riot Grrrl didn't do anything, well, the legacy of the movement is so massive that now there are multiple rock camps for girls all around the United States. At our rock camp, we employ a gentle radical feminism that teaches the girls basic self-confidence and the simple but radical idea that they have the right as young women to access the world of music, or any world they want. We teach them how to read music or, if they choose, to not read music and learn instead through hands-on and intuitive means. We help them learn how to respect one another. We have workshops about gender identity and racism, and in the process we adult teachers are learning as well. Kids don't realize the offhand racist comments they can make, and as a grown-up you have to learn how to address that and know when it's appropriate to intervene and when to just let things play out.

In one way, Rock Camp is even helping me to be a better musician. I have to admit that I didn't know what monitors were for until I was about twenty-four years old. I knew there were these big black speakers facing me up on the stage, but I didn't know I was supposed to hear myself in them. I would blow my voice out on the first three nights of a tour, just screaming, trying to get a sense of what I sounded like. Even now I am just learning to use a PA, and the reason I'm learning is because I've got to teach eight-year-olds how to use a PA! So they are really teaching me, which is hilarious.

At Rock Camp it always comes back to basic self-love and acceptance. When a girl is feeling bummed out about her singing, I want to know if she feels sad because she's been told she's a bad singer her whole life, or because she doesn't sound like her favorite singer, or because she just doesn't like herself. Is she so self-conscious she doesn't really want to be heard, so her natural voice gets strangled and comes out like a dry little squeak? These are questions all singers need to ask themselves. I think the older you get the more comfortable you become in your body, and the more relaxed you are with yourself, the more your natural voice can take shape and stun you.

There is a music library at the camp that allows the girls to learn about music they might not find on their own—not just PJ Harvey and Joan Jett but Ma Rainey and Cibo Matto and Yoko Ono. There are a lot more women of color and fat women involved in music than you would ever know from watching MTV. I like to bring in vocalists who totally challenge the way the girls understand voice. It empowers the kids to see that everyone is capable. That fame isn't the most important goal and that there are many different levels of success. Your definition of success is more important than anyone else's. You're not often taught that what matters in this life is your happiness, and we work to impart this simple philosophy to the girls at Rock Camp.

Teaching at Rock Camp, I made friends with one girl who was

just a natural weirdo, a little kid with a crazy high voice. And not high like a little girl's voice tends to be—it was a powerful, supernatural high voice coming out of this child. When she spoke she spoke normally, but when she sang it was like her voice was wanting to erupt into some lunatic yodel. The people around her were unsure of how to work with her, and the other little girls were especially annoyed by it. I brought in some Nina Hagen and had them all gather around and listen, asking them, *Would you call this singing?* The wild cries of "New York New York" filled the space, and I watched the little yodeler's eyes go huge, and I could tell that for the first time she was hearing something that made sense to her. Not every artist gets to have this moment, where you connect with someone who came before you, who is channeling the same creative energy as you and helps you make sense to yourself. It took me twenty-seven years to get to that moment, and right then, at Rock Camp, I got to have a sneak peek at what it would be like to get that sort of understanding when you're eight or nine years old. And this is why feminism is so important. When you're involved in feminist-oriented projects like Rock 'n' Roll Camp for Girls—or whatever arts festival or political group or zine project you're involved in—it's easy to get lost in the big picture or sidetracked by how much hard work there is. But you've got to remember you're doing it for the Nina Simones and Yoko Onos of the coming generations, so they don't stay ignorant of their own voices and their own creative power in this world. I have a friend whose music teacher wanted to test her for a hearing problem because her sound was so unusual! If she'd been in Rock Camp we'd have just found some raw lady singer who matched up with her natural style, providing her with a role model and a map to her creative self.

Another thing I teach girls at Rock Camp is how to have stage presence and the confidence to use your body. Every other instrument gives you something to hide behind, but singing comes straight out of your physicality, and there is no place to hide. The female body comes under such constant criticism and scrutiny, and this affects a girl when she is up there, being so vulnerable, letting her strong gorgeous weird surprising voice out. Girls are raised being told you have to sing this one way, talk this one way, sit with your legs crossed, stop taking your top off at the swimming pool, start following all these rules, and these social restrictions bleed into art and make it hard for grown women to access the freedom they need to grow as creative people. This is Feminism 101, and it's crucial to get it to girls when they're young so they don't spend half their life unlearning all the bullshit, wasting time they could be spending perfecting their singing or writing or painting. No one takes us when we're nine years old and makes us listen to Yoko Ono, and I say that it is a radical, healing, and simple thing to do.

In the absence of idealistic feminists turning me on to Nina Hagen and Nina Simone in my youth, I stumbled upon other role models in pop culture. I idolized Miss Piggy, the glamorous, bossy femme from *The Muppet Show*. I really, really idolized Mama Cass, who was fat and could sing and be beautiful and famous. I loved Cyndi Lauper so much that I literally believed we were sisters when I was growing up. I was obsessed with Boy George and his glamorous gender and seductive voice. I couldn't figure it out, but I was so drawn to Boy George! I stopped having cable TV in 1986, when our region capitulated to the demands of the local Christian college and banned MTV. My mother, who liked Talking Heads and Black Sabbath, was a young mom, and she figured what was the point in scraping and scrimping to get us cable when there was no MTV? The last thing I saw on MTV before the Man took it away was Michael Jackson and Madonna, and I remained frozen in that musical moment for a long time, having no way to know about what came next. For years I would do Mom's makeup and draw a little Madonna mole on her cheek.

The lessons I come up with at Rock Camp are really outside the box. I'm trying to give those girls access to everything I missed when I was younger. I like to take Antony and the Johnsons and Nina Simone and play them both for the kids and ask them to tell me what gender each singer is. They always get it wrong. Girls are taught to sing high and pretty, like Antony, not low and from the guts like Nina Simone. But we're slowly trying to change that. There are so many things we're not told growing up, and it's our true feminist responsibility to take the truth to the people who need to hear it.

21

So, eventually Gossip had packed it up and left the teeny-weeny town of Olympia for the thriving metropolis of PDX, OR, which was just hours away, but the scene was bigger—more places to play, to live, to eat, to shop. Instead of nine months of solid rain there are only eight!

Portland was stuffed with queers and punks and artists who had fled Olympia once the scene got too stifling. As magical as Olympia was to land in, once you've been there for a few years, as my band and I had, it becomes claustrophobic. The same little one-block downtown, once so quaint, seems tired. You crave newness, a bit of space, the freedom to walk down the street without seeing fifteen people you know in fifteen minutes. There is a fine line between community and feeling socially oversaturated. It was time to move on. We all could feel it—Nathan, Kathy, even, thankfully, Freddie. Nathan and I got a house together, and everyone else found rooms with friends who'd already completed their migration from Olympia to Portland. I was excited for my next chapter and to see what would happen to Gossip out of the cozy confines of our supportive womb. I packed my belongings—mostly clothes and records—into Nathan's car, and we sang songs the whole way down into Oregon.

But soon enough life in my new town started to feel overwhelming. A month or so earlier I had been on tour with Gossip and some scary things had happened with my vision. Everything would just go white, like the cable disconnecting on your television set. Electric snow. I couldn't see anything for a brief moment, and then my vision would return and it would be okay and I'd think, That was weird, and get on with it. That was the tour when I started hearing how skinny I was. *Beth, you look skinny, are you okay?* I'd shrug. *Yeah, I'm fine.*

I wasn't fine. I got to Portland and couldn't stop crying. I missed Jeri something terrible. I'd left my best friend since I was fifteen behind in Olympia, and I hated to be without him. He was and is my absolute support system, and I had no money to call him. Freddie tried to be there for me, but he had his own challenges going on. He was also adjusting to a new town, a new scene. I was waking up at 5:30 and taking the bus to whatever crappy job I'd scored that season. And in the still morning before Portland woke up, before the sun cracked the sky, in the cold and lonely darkness something happened to my brain and I started wanting to die. I started thinking about how I could do it. I could throw myself out of the bus, I would think, wondering how to get a window open. Or in the Gossip van, or a friend's car, I could just pop open the door and hurl myself onto the road.

I had moved from a place where I knew what would happen every single day to one that was more of a city and less of a one-horse town. In Olympia, the buses stopped running at 9:45 P.M. In Portland, the buses ran late, and they crisscrossed the entire startlingly huge city. A city! I was living in an actual city! Go ahead and laugh at me, New Yorkers and Londoners. I had grown up on a glorified dirt road and from there moved to an insular town with a three-block main street. Portland gave me a panic attack.

While Olympia didn't ultimately have very much going on, Portland actually had quite a big scene, or really, lots of smaller scenes that sometimes overlapped and sometimes didn't. I didn't get my driver's license until I was twenty-five, so the buses became my friend as I learned the routes and zigzagged my way around town.

But then, as I was starting to get the hang of my new surroundings, something happened to my body. I became stricken with this mysterious, awful illness. I suddenly needed glasses. I couldn't see anything and I was frighteningly skinny. So skinny that years later Freddie found a photo of me from that moment and wondered, *Who is this girl sitting on my lap—I better not show Beth, she'll get pissed.* It was me. I was so skinny I could fit into a pair of Kathy's pants. It was like one day I woke up and I weighed 140 pounds. This person who had weighed 200 pounds had, for no apparent reason, lost almost half her body weight. I had a funny taste in my mouth all the time, something sickly sweet and wrong.

The fucked-up thing was, I didn't realize I was skinny. I think that growing up fat-empowered gave me another kind of body dysmorphia. I had no idea what was happening to me. I later learned that my weight loss was caused by issues with my gallbladder, and I wound up having my gallbladder removed, but at that moment it was just another mysterious symptom that made me feel like I was losing my mind.

I started cutting myself. I never knew how good cutting could feel until I felt that bad, there in Portland. Until I felt so bad and so numb that the only sensation I could really register was pain. It broke through the dark still cold morning that had leached into my heart and made everything quiet and deadened and numb.

Nighttime was awful. I would have nightmares, dreams of my mom and my uncle and my dad, absolute wretched nightmares. I would wake up crying in the night. I didn't want to fall back asleep and face my imaginings and I didn't want to stay awake in the rotten darkness with my mind so broken and alive.

I got skinnier and skinnier and my vision worsened, and one day I woke up and was snow-blind, like what had happened on tour, only this time it stuck around for terrifying minutes, not just brief, shocking seconds. Imagine how slow a minute creeps by when your vision has been sucked out of your eyeballs. Imagine a whole bunch of snow-blinded minutes, all piled up on one another while you go mad with fear. My vision would begin to tint purple, and then the purple would flare into blinding whiteness and I would fall to the ground. This happened once, and then again and then again and then it happened again. I would scream for whoever was near me, Nathan, Kathy, Freddie. And then my vision would come back and I would try to pretend it hadn't happened. Until it happened again.

In the midst of my falling apart, Freddie and I started to have problems. I was so easily threatened, so easily triggered by everything. Freddie would be having sex with me and I would haul off and punch him in the face for no reason. He was the only person I had to lean on, and he became too exhausted to deal with whatever was taking over my mind and my body.

Freddie wrapped his hand around the thickest part of my arm, gone scrawny. *You are very little,* he told me. *I don't feel little,* I said. I didn't feel little, but my dress size had dropped to 8 and I couldn't see. I went to an eye doctor. He said, *There is something wrong with your eyes, and you need to get it checked out.* He wanted me to go to a specialist. But I didn't have money to go to the doctor, I didn't even have the money to pay him. I took the glasses he prescribed and I never went back.

But it didn't take long for the glasses to stop working. My vision was deteriorating. There was a redness in my eyes, a red ring inside the iris, circling the pupil. I let it all go for about a year, until I couldn't get by without a stronger pair of glasses. I went back to that doctor, still skinny, growing blinder. Half my face was paralyzed; it looked as if I'd had a stroke. I couldn't close my mouth, couldn't drink water unless I tilted my head way back. The palsy would switch sides, immobilizing one half of my face and then the other. The eye doctor was alarmed. *You never went to the specialist.* It wasn't a question. Obviously I hadn't gone.

I'd lost 30 percent of the vision in my right eye. It was so crazy. I still can't see out of it well. In my left ear I had lost 40 percent of my hearing. And now my throat was beginning to malfunction as well. I had tried to eat a donut at work and was horrified to have it come right out my nose. The muscles in my throat had stopped working. It made it so I couldn't swallow, and that made it so that I couldn't talk. Without those muscles your vocal cords can't vibrate, so my voice came out my nose like that donut—tinny, nasal, a scary joke of a voice. I remember when it had first started happening, I'd asked my co-worker if he could hear my voice. He looked at me like I was crazy. *Yeah, I can hear your voice.* But something was wrong, in my voice or in my head. Or maybe I was just losing my mind, or everything at once.

On that second visit to the eye doctor, he said to me, *If you don't go to a specialist right now, you are going to go blind. And if you tell me right now you can't go to the specialist, I am putting you in an ambulance and sending you there.* The eye doctor had looked inside my eyes and found huge growths there. He told me I had this crazy disease called sarcoidosis.

After the specialist was done investigating me, he plopped into his chair and faced me frankly. *If there was time, and I didn't think you would be damaged from the experience, I would call in a fleet of medical students, because I have never seen anything like this in my life.* With sarcoidosis, a special sort of helpful cell my immune system produces gets out of hand, and the cells gang up into massive clusters called granulomas. Then a little strain of microbes, which have learned to thrive inside the granulomas meant to kill them, start multiplying. Hence the creation of yet more granulomas. On and on it goes, a whole crazy war being fought microscopically inside my body. Inside my eyes, inside my brain.

I was apparently the rarest of the rare, such a spectacular case that the doctor fretted about his inability to show me off to the sarcoidosis scholars. Granulomas had formed on my eye, causing part of my pupil to flatten. To have it affect your brain is the most terrifying and terminal situation. The disease causes your brain to tell your organs to stop working. So far my sarcoid gray matter had told my eyes and my throat to call it quits. It had radioed my ears and told them to take a break. It's as if a slow sensory deprivation takes over your body, your brain shutting the systems down, sense by sense. The specialist prescribed me a steroid, a sort of wonder drug that vetoed my brain's orders and restored my body to normal, more or less. Sometimes the sides of my face go numb, and I just wait for the feeling to come back and try not to freak out. And the feeling always comes back.

My friend Lyndell is an amazing hairdresser, and she has recurrent dreams that her hands are cut off and she can never work with hair again, slicing locks into feathering cascades, blunting a bob, building a sculpture with a can of hairspray and a fistful of bobby pins. I tell her I know that fear, having lost the ability to talk. Knowing that the sarcoidosis is there beneath the steroids, that it never goes away. It becomes dormant, and you hope that it stays asleep and docile, but it can always flare up again. Bernie Mac had sarcoidosis in his lungs that went into remission until he got sick with pneumonia, and then it killed him. It is a really, really, really rare disease. And finding out that I had it was what pushed me straight into a nervous breakdown. I had no money, no nothing. I had already been flirting with suicide, and now it seemed that my body was a step ahead of my mind.

I've always been really prone to depression. When I was growing up, it felt like no one in my family wanted me. Well, maybe Aunt Jannie had, but she was such an abusive person, and she up and died anyway. My mom shacked up with a loser. She lied to me about who my real dad was, and I was worried she'd pull a similar deceit on my little sister. I'd been molested since before I could remember and had followed it up with a bunch of abusive sex partners until Anthony. I was totally gay and afraid of hell and afraid of God. I fell in love with my best friend and she started dating my brother. My friends all moved away and I had to choose to either stay behind and get knocked up or be impossibly brave and follow them.

It was Freddie who told me I had to deal with all these feelings I was having, this backed-up lifetime of festering sadness and hurt and betrayal. When you're intimate with someone the way I was with Freddie, you let the other person in so deep he sees everything, things that you can't see. Freddie saw my hurt, my terror, he knew the source of my loneliness, he could connect the dots between the struggles I had today and what I'd survived in Arkansas. As obvious as it was, I couldn't see it. I was too deep in it, drowning in it. He helped me get so much clarity about where my head was at and why, and he gave me the support to start handling it.

I couldn't deal with talking to my mother. I was angry because my younger sister was hitting the same age I was when I'd been left alone in this world of abusive boys who had been so absolutely awful to me. To see her at that age, vulnerable, unprotected, was so triggering to me. And I've got to tell you I hate that word, "triggered." People who use it annoy me. I hate the word, but it explains where I was at, what was happening. My sister was turning that age. The age my cousin was when she let someone know that Dean had raped her. That age. The same awful things had happened to my mom. Kids at school said she was easy and other, worse things. Maybe my mom was trying to protect me by not making a huge deal out of what had happened to me and potentially dragging me through the same sort of courtroom drama she'd experienced, but the lack of action only made me feel like shit and responsible for what I'd lived through. The fear of her repeating that with my little sister made me shake with how powerless I was to do anything. For any of us.

My mother had multiple chances to intervene, to put a stop to my sexual abuse, and she didn't. I woke up with the pain of it every day and went to sleep with it every night. The way my mind was taking my thoughts and weaving them into blankets to smother me, it was killing me, I had to make a change. My mom wasn't going to suddenly come to her senses and try to make up for what she had or hadn't done. No one was going to do that. Freddie couldn't save me. I had to save myself.

Every morning I would wake up and say, *You have to get up. You have to go to work. You have to make your stupid kava kava tea that smells like a rotting birthday cake but calms your nerves enough to get you out the door.* I have a panic attack just at the smell of that tea, which is the opposite of what it's supposed to do for you. I drank and drank that awful tea, but what I really needed was a babysitter. Someone to stop me from cutting the huge gash into my arm. The one so deep I could see the meat of my body. The one that had me thinking, If I can do it this deep I can do it deeper, and if I do it that much deeper I can do it deeper still, and finally I will have the courage to kill myself.

Freddie said to me, *If you die then we all have to live without you.* That little sentence kept me alive. Freddie being angry kept me alive. As for my other friends, they were pretty checked out right around then. Kathy was engaged to marry this guy she didn't want to be with but she couldn't bring herself to tell him. When I told her I was feeling suicidal, she sent me flowers. It was her way of letting me know she loved me. Nathan was off in his own world. It was his girlfriend at the time who took me to the hospital in a cab. That's where you go when you're all grown up and you need a babysitter. I needed a babysitter, badly. And so I went to the hospital.

22

In the hospital I met crazy people. Someone screamed at me, *That bitch with the black hair, I'll kill her!* I was locked inside with that caliber of crazy. People who had been in there for a long time, who had literally not seen the outside in months. People who acted like children, who came up to me in the cafeteria and demanded to know if I was going to finish my hamburger or could they have it.

While I was being babysat, a horrible snowstorm was happening outside. It was like all the drama of my own interior landscape became a weather front manifested in the real world. Things froze, pipes burst, cars skidded all over Portland. People couldn't leave their houses. Power went out. But inside the hospital all ran smoothly, as it always did. The bright overhead fluorescence highlighted the worry wrinkles we'd put on our faces. Our skin was dry from all the salty tears run down it. Stress gave us pimples and our nerves compelled us to pick them. Everyone looked like shit in the hospital.

Once I was there, where I wanted to be, with my babysitters, I got scared. I thought, I am not going to get to go home. The doctors didn't think I was well enough. They would ask me what I thought about my life and I would tell them. I would tell them about Uncle Lee Roy and the three little A's, about punching Freddie and cutting myself. It was always men asking me these questions, never women. Doctors. Women were the nurses, and there was bulletproof glass between the halls I roamed and the rooms they sat in, with their paperwork and their computers.

My roommate was a woman who just lay on her bed all day like a dead person. It was creepy. I would have preferred the screaming woman who wanted to kill me. Every morning at 7:00 we would get woken up to do crafts, or to go to group therapy, and my roommate would just lie there, refusing to participate. After a while they just left her alone. Flat on her back, staring at the ceiling, vacated.

In group therapy there was a man who had thrown himself in front of a car. He'd been there for six months. There was an abuse survivor who was addicted to drugs, and a woman who had so fallen apart her kids had been taken from her. There were people in the circle who could not hold a conversation that went above a twelve-year-old level, and we were all having therapy together. As if you could deal with all of us in the same way!

This is how low I've gotten, I thought; I'm in here with someone who flung himself in front of a car. To hear someone who had actually acted on his suicidal compulsion was a wake-up call. And at the same time, I thought, Of course I'm crazy. This is our support system? This is the babysitter? This is where people who survive rape and incest wind up? No one in the hospital was looking at our abuse from a feminist perspective. There was no feminism in the hospital, there was no queer-positivity. Up until that point I had never really cried. I had cried right after Aunt Jannie died, but that's it. Now, in the hospital, I couldn't stop crying. I cried for me and for my little cousins and for my sister and my mother and for the women in group therapy and the woman who wanted to kill me and the woman who wouldn't get out of bed and the man who threw himself under the moving car. I cried and I cried and I thought, Well, maybe this is why I'm here. Maybe I had to find a place where I could finally cry. I'd driven Freddie to the end of his rope, till he had had enough and couldn't take it anymore. I had reached out to my friend and she'd given me flowers. Jeri was so far away; no one had cars or money for a long-distance phone call. All I wanted was to be held twenty-four hours a day. And people can't do that. They can't hold you twenty-four hours a day. I knew that I needed to die or I needed to live, and I just needed a minute to figure out which. And to cry.

Freddie came to visit me twice. I was only released because he had come to get me. They wouldn't let me leave alone, not in the terrible snow, which had not let up. I left the whiteness of the institution for the sharp, pretty whiteness of the outside. There was real air there, and I sucked it into my lungs. The snow felt like cold little kisses on my face. The gray sky felt gentle after the harsh lights that striped the ceiling of that hospital. A friend of Freddie's who was in a queercore band called the Third Sex was sitting in the driver's seat of the car outside, the motor running, steam from the snow rising up around her shaking car.

I had only been in the hospital for four days, but it seemed like forever. I felt changed from those hours, I felt like my life had shifted somehow, was different. The doctors had put me on Lexapro; one of the side effects was yawning and I was yawning once a minute, I swear. Ask Nathan. He could hardly be around me, because yawning is so contagious and I'd yawn and he'd yawn and I'd yawn again and it was yawning madness. The Lexapro wasn't working. It made me so anxious I lay in bed like my psych ward roommate, my teeth chattering. It was awful, it made everything worse. They switched me to Prozac, and that started working. I took it all the time. But I hated the long, long walk to get my prescription filled. I always had this thing I internalized, how people think fat people are lazy, and in my heart I was scared I was like that, lazy, so lazy I didn't even want to get up and get my own medicine. But really, I just needed help. I needed someone to be there to make sure I took my medicine. My babysitter. I still needed that babysitter so bad.

I moved through it every day. My panic, my sadness, my exhaustion. When it got real bad I called Akasha. She said to me, *Beth, if you can't take it week by week, you take it day by day. If you can't take it hour by hour, you take it minute by minute, and if that doesn't work you take it second by second, but you take it.* And that totally worked. Because it came from her. Because she knew how I grew up, and she knew what I was struggling with. And because she is not a woman of words, Akasha, so for her to come out with all that meant a lot. One of her favorite sayings is "Why would I write in a card, the card says it better than I do. The card says it all." She says this every time she sends you a card, and then you get it in the mail with the little flourish of her signature and that's it.

And so I knew I had to take my own steps toward happiness. I thought a lot about my sister's advice: *week, day, hour, minute, second.* Taking it. The steps I have to take to stay sane. You have to go through the pain of things to heal them.

23

In 2005, Kathy left Gossip. It was heartbreaking. Our lives—
Gossip's life, and Kathy's life—were going in two very different
directions. It was the saddest moment the band had ever had. The
instability of life in a band had hit its peak for Kathy, and she
needed a job. A real job, one she could rely on, one that was constant and guaranteed. Nathan and I were so used to being unstable, we didn't even notice it, and while Kathy had had her own instability growing up, she's a Virgo and wasn't interested in bringing childhood patterns of shaky scarcity into her adult life. Kathy
needs stability, a rock; she's earth, she needs to be grounded. It is
not a grounding experience, being in a quasi-underground punk
band.

While Kathy was grappling with her own experience of practical instability, I found myself at the mercy of my own emotional
instability. After surviving my second nervous breakdown, after
surviving hospitalization, I decided that my life needed to have a
serious direction. And what could my purpose be if not Gossip?
I would rededicate myself to touring and making music my life.

The intense energy it took to relocate to a new city, and the time spent getting back on my feet, had taken my focus away from the band. *Movement* hadn't even been out for a year yet; we'd been on a tour and had a live album just come out, *Undead in NYC*. We'd even started on a new album, writing a bunch of songs that had felt so promising and inspiring, but everything got put on hold while the band settled into Portland and I settled into myself. We hadn't all gotten together to practice in months. I was used to practicing all the time back in Olympia, and I didn't like how far away music felt from me. And now especially, on the heels of such intense instability, I needed something I knew I could rely on. If my own life was something I couldn't get behind 100 percent, I would put my energy into the service of this band that had made me so happy and see if that couldn't keep me alive.

As if the universe itself wanted to confirm that I had made the right choice, Le Tigre invited us to go on tour with them. I was finally going to have my chance to meet Kathleen Hanna! But Kathy said no. She couldn't handle another tour, the instability of it, having to return home and patch her life back together again. Her commitment to living that way was zero. And so Nathan and I had to tell her that we had to move on without her. You could say that we kicked her out of the band, but it didn't feel like that. For us it was a choice between Gossip or keeping our pizza job, or our McDonald's job, because that was all we had going for us outside our music life. Seriously—Nathan was working at McDonald's. For me the choice was clear—I would rather be unstable in a band and tour all the time than be depressed in Portland, working at shitty places for shitty money. We made it our goal to be on the road as much as possible, and Kathy could not get behind it.

It just doesn't work to keep getting these jobs and then having to quit them all the time, Kathy said. And she was right. It had become tedious, and at this point we'd gotten and then abandoned jobs all over town. It was harder, upon each return, to find a place we hadn't screwed over already. Kathy's plan was to tour less. My and

Nathan's way of solving the problem was to stay on tour as much as possible. We made a compromise: we'd find a drummer for the tour and then check back in when it was done.

It was so awful to have to give someone you love so dearly, someone who had been the most integral part of this creation, the very person who had invited me to step behind the mic and try to sing—to have to give her an ultimatum, to communicate that we would move on without her. It made me feel so cold, so ruthless. I plummeted into the conversation like jumping from a bridge. Nathan just sat there, and I did all the talking. Sometimes people—even people in the band—forget that Gossip is a group effort. It's not just me, even though I'm the one with the biggest mouth. Nathan even made buttons once that read GOSSIP IS A BAND. It's just the way people read the singer of a band as its leader, which gets encouraged by the fact that I am not a quiet person. So during our breakup conversation with Kathy, I talked my head off and Nathan sat there, mostly quiet. I just understood that if I agreed to have Gossip turn down the Le Tigre tour in order for Kathy to be able to stay at her job, then I would be putting her needs before my own, and I'd simply had it with putting other people before myself. It's one thing to be a compassionate person, and a caring person, and to show up for your friends and help out, but it is another thing entirely to allow another person's wants to determine the course of your destiny. And so Kathy left the band.

Kathy had written "Standing in the Way of Control" with us. She had written "Yr Mangled Heart" with us. She had written that album, had worked on it and made it the hit it became. When we signed with a major label I was adamant about her getting a chunk of money. When we got a publishing deal that included the sale of our records I made sure she got money for that too. I didn't want to become something I hate, the person whose band makes it and they rip off the folks who'd helped them get to that level. I needed Kathy to be taken care of. There would be no Gossip without her. If there was any debt that was owed to her financially I made sure

we paid it and that when she left she left with a clean slate, nothing shady, feeling as good as she could about something that was
in fact pretty awful.

But I couldn't blame Kathy for wanting what she wanted. Right
then, there was no way to know we wouldn't just fall on our faces.
But whether we took off like a bottle rocket or went down in a blaz-
ing minivan of glory, one thing was a sure bet: I was going to get
to meet Kathleen Hanna! My Riot Grrrl heroine whose screamy
voice I longed for mine to sound like, the reluctant leader of the
badass pack. By her thirties, Kathleen Hanna had become a bona
fide living legend, and she just kept moving forward with one
awesome inspiration after another. From Bikini Kill to Julie Ruin,
where she posed as a feminist librarian and made crazy electric
beats. Now Le Tigre, dance sensations whose lyrics and beats were
charged with overt political messages, whether they were shouting out to ignored feminist writers or weaving live antiwar protest
samples into their beats. I could not believe our latest burst of
good fortune.

I never looked at touring with Le Tigre as a great business opportunity. If we were looking for a way to weasel into the industry
like that, we would have toured with Pearl Jam or the Red Hot
Chili Peppers. And believe me, it's not that I dislike or distrust
those bands, but I don't think the people who listen to them are
my people. It's hard to play to crowds who couldn't care less, or
who are potentially super rude to women. I'm just not willing to
put myself in that situation. I wanted to tour with a band I loved
and whose audience would get Gossip and love us, and that was Le
Tigre. And it was a chance to meet Kathleen Hanna! I am shamelessly starstruck by that woman and was not even going to try to
play it cool.

But before we went on tour, we had to find a drummer. Nathan and I racked our brains, trying to come up with Gossip's next
member. Someone punk, we both agreed. And I couldn't be in a
band with two boys, so it had to be a female person. Hannah Blilie

had been playing drums in the band Shoplifting, which had put something out on Kill Rock Stars. Shoplifting had also worked to start a Bands Against Bush chapter in Seattle, organizing other bands and musicians to agitate against the U.S. government. We asked her to fill in for Kathy just for this tour. But as it turned out, Hannah was willing to tour all the time. And when we got back, Kathy had decided to return to school.

So many bands break up because of college. Nathan and I were united in our total lack of interest in higher education. College was just not something I'd ever cared about. Nothing I've ever wanted to do has required schooling, except maybe hairdressing, and I have all the time in the world to do that if I choose. Hannah was into being on the road and living the life of a traveling musician. And we could keep coming back to Kathy, but there was no way Kathy was going to suddenly turn her beat around and want to jump back onto the SS *Unstable* with me and Nathan, and so we soon invited Hannah to be a real member of Gossip. If I was going to take care of myself and patch together the life I wanted, then my band needed a committed, touring drummer. Nathan agreed.

It's crazy the ups and downs we had had together, the three of us—me, Nathan, and Kathy. Though Kathy was the only one to call it quits, at various points it had been hard on us all, the instability and the poverty and the never knowing if anything was ever going to happen. During one era it was Nathan who was halfway about to quit the band, with some deranged plan to move to Canada, and Kathy and I dragged him back into it. Kathy and I are not visual people, and it's always been Nathan who's done the band's graphics and album art. That is Nathan's jam 100 percent. He had moved away to Vancouver to be with a girlfriend, and Kathy and I were struggling trying to put together some album art that didn't look like it was made by a first-grader going wild with a jug of finger paints. This was back right before *Movement* came out. Kathy and I had tried to pull it together without him. Kathy, who came from no money, had splurged her savings on our van. We even tried getting a new guitar player. Finally he saw that we were serious, that we weren't going to quit the band just because he got bored and fell off. So he came back down from Canada and we were a trio again.

When Kathy left the band it became less fun and more serious, which changed things for the better and for the boringer, because you can't go back to touring in a borrowed minivan with a couple of coolers and a Hamburger full of luggage strapped to the roof. Or sleeping on people's floors. Or going blind with undiagnosed sarcoidosis while taking a shower at a stranger's house and having to scream, *Kathy! Kathy!* until she comes in and finds you there spread-eagled in the tub. That was the kind of shit we had gone through together. It was so sad. But Kathy is still making music in bands. Right now she's in one called Manimal. Jeri and I want her to rename it Kathy's Magic Moments, but she won't pay us any mind.

24

After Kathy left, the drum parts for "Standing in the Way of Control" were completely changed. Up until that song, we had never taken ourselves seriously as songwriters. I remember, the minute we were done recording it, looking at Nathan and saying, *Wow. This is it. We wrote an actual song.*

The thing about Gossip is we never planned for any of this to happen, so everything that comes along is like a huge surprise, really unbelievable. And when "Standing in the Way of Control" was written we were just like, *Wow, we wrote a grown-up song. Wow. Wow!* We knew it was special. At the time we thought it was special because it was so mature of us, not because it was good. We just knew we had shifted our music in a new direction, and that alone was exciting.

When we were talking to Kill Rock Stars about *Standing in the Way of Control,* they told us our budget was going to change. Cool, we thought. But it leapt from a seven-thousand-dollar budget to a twenty-five-thousand-dollar budget. To us that was crazy incredible. No one had ever dealt with a figure like twenty-five thousand dollars before. Not one of us, not even our parents. When we heard about a twenty-five-thousand-dollar budget just for our recording costs, we were ecstatic, but we didn't exactly know what it would mean.

It meant we could take ten whole days to make our record. It meant we got to record in this really amazing barn that had been converted into a studio. James Brown had recorded there, as had all these grunge bands. It was in the woods outside Seattle. There was a loft and a kitchen, it was a hotel/studio, and we got so much work done because we could just play music and write songs all night. "Listen Up!" came from an all-night songwriting bender. It was very cool, and we were very lucky. I did get a little stir crazy, because I didn't have a driver's license and couldn't get myself out of the woods, but it was springtime so the woods were really nice and everything was pretty much perfect. We had a giant budget and were working with Guy Picciotto from Fugazi. That was such a big deal for us. He is a great person—a truly gentle man and a part of punk history that we look up to. It was surreal and unbelievable and we felt blessed. We never knew we could have our songwriting process be so crazy and inspired. When we got to the studio we had four songs written, and by the end of ten days we had created an album.

The only example I ever had of a successful band is one that went on tour, paid its bills, and broke even. That was the only example any of us ever had, and so that was our goal. No one had ever thought this record would go to the Top 40 in the U.K., or that we'd ever rack up gold records. There is a gold record hanging on the wall of the double-wide trailer Mom lives in today. How crazy is that? Fucking crazy is how crazy. I bet it is heavier than her whole house. All we had wanted to do is all we ever want to do: make a better record than our last one. Or make a different record than our last one. That it ended up doing so well, having mainstream crossover, was crazy and absurd and none of us saw it coming.

It's been hard to understand our success in Europe, because we don't live there, and so I miss a lot of it. We got to be on TV shows, but it didn't stick out for me because I had never seen those TV shows. So we would get an amazing invitation, and I would think it was no big deal. We had played *The Jonathan Ross Show*—he's the David Letterman of England. When we eventually played David Letterman's show, I knew what that meant. I knew it was *The Late Show* and that it didn't get any bigger for a band playing on TV. And that's what was happening with *The Jonathan Ross Show*, but I couldn't gauge it. Everything was unreal. It wasn't until I did the second cover for the *NME*—the naked cover—that I realized that we had become famous.

The year the *NME* voted me the coolest person in rock was the first year the world's coolest person was a woman. It was also the first time they didn't put the world's coolest person on the cover. I caused a big stink about it. Later they put Gossip on the cover. Eventually they were like, we want Beth on the cover, and we want her to be completely naked. I mulled it over for a long time, not because I didn't want to be naked, but because I knew I would be opening myself up to a lot of criticism. Not only comments about my body, but I was sure people would be questioning my motives, as if I were somehow incapable of making the decision to pose naked for myself. There's a lot of value in polarizing imagery. The hysteria and furor over something as simple and common as a fat female body tells us a lot about where our culture is at with issues of sexism and body politics. Ninety-five percent of the time, I don't mind being made fun of. You can call me fat, just don't say I can't sing. I know I can sing! And so I did it. I was even on my period, and I did it. It was painless—I'm okay with being naked, it's not a big deal. They put a lot of makeup on my body, and they put all these giant kiss marks all over me. That wasn't my favorite thing, but the more photo shoots you do, the more you see that this is their art, and you have to trust them. So I was like, Okay, here I go! I trusted them.

Though I'm far removed from Britain, the photo has been re-printed lots of places, so I've seen it a bunch. What got a lot more flack than me being fat and naked was my armpit hair! I don't go digging around for criticism, but sometimes you can't help but run into it. Someone said, *It's bad enough she's nude, can't she shave her armpits?* I was not really surprised by this. In a culture where people look at an image on TMZ or whatever for 0.5 seconds be-fore posting the first comment that pops into their heads, layered, contextual analysis of pop culture imagery pretty much falls by the wayside. Overall, though, the response was positive, and it was something I could be proud of. It was also nominated as maga-zine cover of the year! If anything, it has shock value. You can't *not* look at it.

The interviewer for the *NME*, James Jam—who I love!—said to me, *Well, you know, you are a celebrity.* And I said, *No, I don't feel like a celebrity.* I have a huge reality check called the United States. I come home and it's very normal. I have a neighbor who goes to work at a nursing home at night and comes home and babysits during the day, and that's how she makes her money. My other neighbors across the street are on disability. It's always rainy. It's not like my immediate life changed with all this fame, it was like my life in Britain changed, and that's all the way across the ocean! But James Jam said, *You are. You are a celebrity.* And I said, *Maybe I should start taking this seriously. Maybe I should start being more careful.*

Let's get totally real about it and say that it's not just taste that keeps Gossip ignored by U.S. media. It's sexism, the way women who are outspoken about all the real bullshit females deal with in this world either get ignored or made into jokes. I mean, even when I made the *NME*'s Cool List, Gossip's hometown paper didn't mention it. I didn't know I'd won till a journalist called,

asking how I felt about it. He said, *You're number one!* And that's
when everything really began. Whenever we got asked to do anything we were just shocked and grateful. We still are. I'm really
uncomfortable with the word "celebrity," but at a certain point I
had to accept it. Suddenly I was trying to just have a cigarette on a
London street, like a normal person, and I noticed all these people
with cameras swarming around and realized—too late—that they
were taking pictures of me. It's so weird. I always wonder, Why
don't you go and take pictures of someone who matters! James
Jam woke me up to the reality I'd been resisting, that I've reached
for-real celebrity status. He asked me, *If you're getting pictures
taken of yourself hanging out with Kate Moss, don't you think that
makes you a celebrity?* It woke me up to the fact that, if I'm walking
red carpets, it's time to face and accept the fame that makes me so
uncomfortable. And I always get to go home to Portland, Oregon,
when it's over, where the media ignores me! It's very humbling.

I know not to look for things written about me in the press. I literally never read them. The backlash of Gossip's success, the things
that get written about me—it's not about the music anymore, it's
about me, and how I'm "overweight" and wear tight clothes. But
I never said that all I cared about was music, and truly it is just as
important for me to be "overweight" and wearing tight clothes. To
be myself in this world is every bit as important and radical as any
song I've ever sung.

But it is hard sometimes to be taken seriously—hard even for
me to take myself seriously. I am such a wacky person, and if you
add fat to wacky you are doubly doomed. I think it is hard for some
people to take you seriously, and so they treat you like a walking
joke. My approach to fat politics has always been to change people's minds from the inside out. I've always been into connecting
with normal people in a normal way, even if what we're talking

about is a sort of radical concept. It shouldn't still be a surprise to read a review or critique of Gossip and find that it is actually about my body, but it is. It still surprises me, so I avoid them. Before the band blew up, I would walk into shows with Kathy and everyone would assume that Kathy was the singer, because she is so conventionally pretty. People who looked like me just weren't the singer, even in Riot Grrrl scenes. Most all the singers in Riot Grrrl bands always had something more traditionally pretty about them.

Being fat has given me a different perspective on art and beauty, on what is meaningful and beautiful. I never looked up to Marilyn Monroe, I looked up to Miss Piggy and Divine and Mama Cass and Leigh Bowery. My role models—when I finally found them—were so much about approaching meaning, appearances, and life from a radical place, and it is just as important to me to stand among them like that as it is to make another record. I only ever wanted to be a singer. And as hard as it was to find my place and my role models and examples there was always that quote: "It's not over till the fat lady sings." That's pretty cool. That means something. The fat lady sings. But it's not nearly over. We are out there bringing punk philosophy to the people and expanding people's definitions of acceptable images and behavior.

For instance, once we were dropped by a booking agent in the rudest way—he didn't even tell us! He'd just stopped booking our tour. I was on the phone with him, telling him, *This is not punk, you don't treat people this way!* Punk to me has always been a moral philosophy, more than a style of music or a fashion you wear. The underpinnings of all the songs and clothes was, for me, a core rejection of the way the world operates, the mainstream world. It was a critique of capitalism, which makes some people rich on the backs of so many powerless workers. It was about smashing beauty standards that taught fat girls and boys and anyone not adhering to inhuman expectations to hate themselves. It was about challenging racism, challenging homophobia. And when you get down to what all these rebellions have in common, it's basic kindness. Love, even. It is making a pledge not to hurt other people—not to profit off their labor, not to teach them to hate their bodies, not to turn hostile at the way we differ from one another, but to go forward, toward a giant community, fighting only against whoever would keep us down and apart, powerless. Under the whole "personal is political" motto of feminism, I feel that personal kindness, treating people decently, is political—is punk. So this incident with the booking agent, though it might seem like no big whoop, was one of my biggest wake-ups. Not everyone has punk ethics.

25

If the ten days we had to record *Standing in the Way of Control* seemed luxurious, we were about to have our minds blown by working with producer Rick Rubin on the next record. Rick gives nary a shit about a budget. His whole approach to being in the studio was totally relaxed and unstressed. He was about giving us time and space to experiment. There wasn't the pressure of feeling like we had a handful of days to get everything done; we were able to take the time to try out things we wouldn't have otherwise. For this record, we had signed to Sony. There's an idea that working with a major label means you give up creative control, but our experience recording with Rick was just the opposite—he really provided an environment that made us feel loved and supported, as if the emphasis was on the process rather than cranking out the product in as little time as possible.

We recorded at Shangri-La Studios in Malibu. It's a weird little compound, a long ranch building with a studio in one half and the owner's house in the other and a handful of outbuildings. One of them is a moldy old Airstream-ish tour bus formerly belonging to Bob Dylan (boring), which Nathan sat in alone for hours at a time messing around with keyboard parts. Shangri-La is one of the only recording studios I've ever been in that had windows and actual sunlight, and with the property overlooking the Pacific Ocean it was a pretty idyllic environment. Recording means a lot of repetition, a lot of trying things out, listening, then trying again and again. A lot of takeout food and coffee and late nights. But we were lucky to have an amazing team to record with, including the brilliant recording engineer Greg Fidelman, and they kept things as fun as possible.

Malibu pretty much only has surf motels or David Geffen's gruesomely overpriced luxury hotel, so we didn't stay in town. Which is fine with me—Malibu is a town where there are NO DONUTS! Not a single donut shop, and believe me, we looked! Your only donut options are basically Starbucks or box donuts from the grocery store. Which became my food obsession while recording. Powdered Donettes and orange juice. Genius! Every morning we would drive a rented minivan from our hotel over a twisty mountain road lined by rich people's houses. Listening to Grace Jones's "Williams' Blood" on repeat for inspiration, or working on our future side career of writing country songs. I'm dead serious—Nathan and I grew up with the genre and can bust out hilarious rhymes playing off each other. Garth Brooks, we've already written your next jam! Recording is fun and exciting and lonely and scary all at the same time, and these small rituals that develop over the course of working on a record really help get you through it.

After three months, the record was ready to be released out into the world. As with any project that you work on so closely for so long, there were parts I loved and parts I would do differently if I could go back. But it was an exciting moment, not knowing what would happen next, letting it go.

· · ·

And that was the beginning of another year's worth of firsts. My first fashion week—complete with meeting Karl Lagerfeld and Vivienne Westwood and getting to see some of my favorite designers' shows in person. My first house, a little place in the same neighborhood where all my friends live, bought over the phone during that same fashion week. And eventually, buying my mom her first house, moving her out of her falling-down trailer! My first fashion line, getting to watch what seemed like magic as the drawings I gave to the designers at Evans came back as real live shoes, dresses, and tops! It was so amazing to get to make clothes that were exclusively for fat girls, to finally put everything I've learned over the years about dressing my body to work making things for other people to enjoy! Gossip's first platinum records . . . WTF? Venue capacities that were firsts for us, each milestone size more perplexingly big than the last. My first time walking a runway, thanks to the extremely sweet and hilarious John Paul Gaultier. First time playing the Cannes Film Festival. Shooting the first cover of Katie Grand's gorgeous *Love* magazine. Our first time playing Coachella and meeting my longtime idol John Waters!

Eventually truly crazy situations like these start seeming less weird, which is its own kind of weird. I don't know who I'll be meeting next in what strange locale. I don't know how long Gossip will be getting to ride this excellent wave that has brought us out of our snug scene in Olympia and into the giant world. Don't know when I'll find myself over it, the travel and the pressure, and run off to fulfill my other dream of being a hairdresser instead.

Right now, I'm in a good place; I might be halfway around the world, but I have my house to come home to. Portland might have felt like the big city when I showed up there years ago, but after everyplace I've been since, it feels cozy as a hug, the place where my closest friends—my chosen family—live. I always have that, no matter what. I have the places I came from and all the shit I've been through built up inside me like the cells of my body, holding me together, making me who and what I am, and that is permanent too. Nobody in this life knows what is in store for them, and all I have to do is crane my head back and see where I've been to know that anything is possible. And I know that who I am is a product of everything I've survived—all the good and the bad of my past. My gifts and blessings can't be separated from my hardships and curses. It's all one life, and I would not trade it for something different. I have Judsonia so deep beneath my fingernails all the mani-pedis in the world won't dislodge it. I'm my mother's daughter, no matter how imperfectly we've loved each other. I'm Akasha's sister, and I know that without her quiet, constant strength I'd be dead. And I feel connected to all this, whenever I step onto a stage and see the impossibly huge crowd screaming, having come to hear me sing. To say I'm grateful sounds trite. It's like I've won some crazy fucking lottery, and the prize has been my life.

My biggest priorities are to keep being creative in every way I can, which includes playing with my friends' hair, putting together a lunatic outfit, acting stupid with friends—all the stuff that I love doing. I want to keep using this crazy life of mine as a way to change the world, but not in some major way like I'm going to solve world hunger or achieve world peace or something. What I want is the same thing everyone wants, the same thing you want—to hurl myself into this world and trust that it will catch me. That we all belong, and we'll all find the places and the people we'll belong to. I know we all have different magic inside us, and it's up to you to figure what yours might be. Maybe your magic is looking fabulous, maybe it's organizing a protest, maybe it's making a zine or starting a band or helping your friends' band go on their first tour. Take your inspiration and let it lead you out into the world, into your big amazing genius life. Voices in your head, echoes of people trying to hold you down—tell them to fuck off. You're perfect the way you are. You don't need to change anything but the world, so get to it.

ABOUT THE AUTHORS

BETH DITTO was born and raised in Judsonia, Arkansas. She is the lead singer of the band Gossip and lives in Portland, Oregon.

MICHELLE TEA is a memoirist, novelist, and poet. She lives in San Francisco.

ABOUT THE TYPE

This book was set in Scala, a typeface designed by Martin Majoor in 1991. It was originally designed for a music company in the Netherlands and then was published by the international type house FSI FontShop. Its distinctive extended serifs add to the articulation of the letterforms to make it a very readable typeface.